Transcending the Modern Mission Tradition

Transcending the Modern Mission Tradition

Michael Stroope

First published 2020 by Regnum Books International

Regnum is an imprint of the Oxford Centre for Mission Studies
St. Philip and St. James Church
Woodstock Road, Oxford OX2 6HR, UK
www.ocms.ac.uk/regnum

09 08 07 06 05 04 03 7 6 5 4 3 2 1

This is an abridged version of *Transcending Mission: The Eclipse Of A Modern Tradition* (IVP/Apollos, 2017), and used with permission.

British Library Cataloguing in Publication Data. A catalogue record for this book is available from the British Library.

Unless otherwise noted, all Scripture quotations are from the *New American Standard Bible*, La Habra, CA: The Lockman Foundaiton, 1977.

ISBN: 978-1-506476-82-7

eBook ISBN: 978-1-506476-83-4

Typeset in Candara by Words by Design.

Photo by JR Korpa on Unsplash .

The publication of this volume is made possible through the financial assistance of Evangelisches Missionswerk.

Distributed by 1517 Media in the US and Canada

Contents

To Students Past and Present

For Lilias, Silas, Micah, Violet, and Ian

I am deeply grateful to Professor David Cranston for his brilliant surgery on Transforming Mission: The Eclipse of a Modern Tradition. *He has converted its long, rambling argument into a succinct and persuasive call to reimagine afresh the church's faithful witness.*

Prologue

Why a book about the language of mission? Isn't *doing* mission much more important than talking about it? Yet a book about the language of mission is important because our talk about mission determines *who we are* and *what we do*. My encounter with mission language as a young person included images of exotic places and words from heroic figures. These came to me by way of vivid stories and colorful pictures presented by visiting missionaries. What I did not realize was that the rhetoric of mission was highly ambiguous. My seminary studies were challenged by competing images and accounts of what mission meant and how it operated. Even more difficult to reconcile were historical accounts where representatives of mission conquered, coerced, and destroyed in the name of Christianity. During and after seminary studies I remained mission-enthused, but these early questions never disappeared.

A further assault on my understanding of mission came during missionary service in Sri Lanka, where after centuries of mission work, the church was still foreign and divided along the identities of the various colonial powers. Mission had bequeathed imported brands of Christianity. Even though the colonial mission legacy raised perplexing questions and doubts, I carried on as a missionary in Sri Lanka. I remained committed to mission but was no longer as certain of its meaning. After my first term in Sri Lanka, I began doctoral studies in the United States. My intention was to explore how best to evangelize Sri Lankans. However, after discovering Karl Barth and the language of *missio Dei*, I changed my focus and completed a dissertation on Karl Barth's doctrine of God. *Missio Dei* gave me a way to address my growing confusion, allowing me to talk with some comfort and theological reason about mission.

A few years after completing my doctoral studies, David Bosch's *Transforming Mission* made its appearance. I read Bosch, and my small difficulty with mission became a big problem. The new word "'mission'," he concludes on page 233, "is historically linked with the colonial era," yet up to this point he consistently employs "mission" and "missionary" in his discussions of Matthew, Luke, Acts, and Paul, and descriptions of early church, monks, and monasteries. He admits to being anachronistic, and then attempts to redeem mission, but instead he compounds the confusion and perpetuates a problem, and this sent me on a quest. At the center of this investigation are questions of mission's use and aim, origin and meaning. Is "mission" even biblical? If so, then what does it mean? If not, when did the church begin using mission language and why? And what baggage might mission bring into its Christian use from those extra-biblical sources?

Introduction: The Enigma of Mission

Mission is ubiquitous. Mission is enigmatic. In everyday speech, popular and academic books, tweets, and blogs, mission is a common word with a seemingly obvious and straightforward meaning. Yet, upon closer inspection, in its many specialized and technical uses the meaning of "mission" is not at all clear.

Mission operates chiefly as noun and adjective and only occasionally as verb. As a noun, mission has a wide variety of meanings: action, organization, task or duty, building, delegated groups of people, and vocation. Its meaning as a verb is narrow and defined, specifying action performed for a task. And as an adjective, it modifies and qualifies structures, places, and activities. Rather than a shallow and clear stream, mission is a wide and deep river. The result is a word that causes a great deal of confusion and hides a host of currents in its depths.

The oldest and most common use of mission is as a political or diplomatic term. The national and political interests of one country or territory are represented to another country or territory through its diplomatic mission. Representatives of a mission travel from one country to another to communicate ideals, negotiate agreements, and protest actions. The ambassador of one country takes up residence in another and establishes an embassy, consulate, or mission.

In contemporary life, the use of mission is everywhere. Companies and organizations, from IBM and General Electric to the Girl Scouts, Starbucks, and the United States Marines, employ the term to describe who they are and what they do. Mission is more than a product. Mission is a way of operating their company and their path to success. It is an essential component of a serious business plan.

The world of personal development offers yet another context and meaning for mission, stressing the necessity of successful persons having a mission, expressed in a personal mission statement. Mission describes the way one frames existence and provides motivation for success. Since the middle of the twentieth century, many people associate mission with the National Aeronautics and Space Administration (NASA). Mission is exploration and endeavors.

For most of us, mission expresses vocation, purpose, or a particular task, whether in sports and business conversations, in everyday and academic settings, and by the religious as well as non-religious, it is everywhere and used by everyone.

In contrast to these routine uses of mission, in the narrow Christian sense, it refers to a definite set of ideas, processes, activities, identities, organizations, strategies, and documents that relate to the advance of Christianity. And yet, even when restricted to its specialized Christian use, the waters do not become clearer: in fact, they become murkier. For most Christians, mission is simply the effort to address the human condition, proselytize others, and spread the Christian faith. But, for a narrow group of religious professionals, mission is seen as a specialty, or even a science, with its own community of practitioners and scholars who use insider technical language and conduct specialized discussions. Missionaries and missiologists discuss and debate mission strategies, missionary methods, mission theology, and a myriad of other topics that fall within "missiology." And yet, even among these specialists, the meaning of mission is varied and contested.

For some it is narrowly defined as "evangelism that results in churches," restricting it to the conversion of non-Christians to the faith and to preaching, evangelism, and church planting. At the other extreme are those who employ mission as the alternative or counterpoint to evangelism, and thus, in some cases, mission is everything but evangelism. Thus, mission means anything and everything the church does, from discipleship to eldercare, building homes through Habitat for Humanity to disaster relief in cooperation with the Red Cross. For those within mainline strands of Protestantism, particularly in the World Council of Churches, mission could include political and social action, as well as peace-making, reconciliation, and healing in the context of brokenness. Salvation, conferred through mission efforts, means the improvement of the common life, redemption of societal structures, and humanization of systems that alienate and destroy.

Evangelicals, such as John Stott and Samuel Escobar, also have broadened the definition of mission to include more than proclamation and conversion. Stott asserts that mission is "a comprehensive word, embracing everything which God sends his people into the world to do. It therefore includes evangelism and social responsibility, since both are authentic expressions of the love which longs to serve man in his need" (35). Escobar insists that in order to avoid a "dualistic spiritualization" that is so prevalent among

Evangelicals, mission must be defined as relating "to every area of human need." Mission must be holistic (105). Christopher Wright expands "mission" to include care for the whole of creation *and* a call to conversion, addressing both disease such as combating HIV and planting churches (412-20, 433-39). The more inclusive definition of mission by Stott, Escobar, and Wright, has on the one hand been vigorously opposed by more conservative detractors and, on the other hand, been critiqued by those within mainline Christianity as not going far enough.

Then there are those Christians, usually of the younger generation, who do not care for the church's mission language at all and refuse to use it. Their objection is most often based either on a lack of emotional connection with mission as evidenced in previous generations, or they see mission as belonging to an era that has long since passed. It is tainted by colonialization and Western imperialism.

To illustrate the breadth of meaning in the word, and thus, the extent of its problem, I differentiate below seven possible meanings of mission and provide statements representative of each. As can be seen, the meaning of mission varies and how each of these is expressed differs per the context and speaker.

> **M1** Mission as general, common task of representation or personal assignment
>
> *a) Elizabeth has made it her mission to make sure all the children in the area are able to attend school.*
>
> *b) The mission of the soldiers is to take control of the tower.*
>
> **M2** Mission as specified aim or goal of a corporate entity

a) The mission of our company is to provide products of superior quality and value that improve the lives of consumers all over the world.

b) The mission of International Justice Mission is to combat human trafficking.

M3 Mission as specific and personal life purpose or calling

a) My mission in life is to raise three children and provide hospitality for those who enter my home.

b) God called me to mission work in Japan when I was ten years old.

M4 Mission as evangelism and church planting

a) Mission means proclamation of the gospel to those who have never heard it.

b) Mission is evangelism that results in new converts and churches.

M5 Mission as the ministry of the church in all its forms

a) The ministries of the church contribute to the accomplishment of its overall mission.

b) The mission of Shady Oaks Baptist Church is to make disciples through all of its activities.

M6 Mission as structures or entities related to the expansion of Christianity

a) Mission San Juan Capistrano was established in 1776 by Spanish Catholics of the Franciscan order.

b) A mission was established across the border as a base for Christian witness in the surrounding area.

M7 Mission as the activity of God in the world, often with little to no reference to the church

a) God's mission is much larger and often different from the work of the church.

b) Mission is the function of the kingdom of God in world history.

While there are undoubtedly more definitions and examples, these seven represent the broadest and most common uses of "mission" by Christians. The first three usages (M1-M3) occur in both secular and religious contexts and can mean something quite different in each. A secular use of M3 communicates that whatever one is doing gives purpose and meaning to life. On the other hand, a religious use of M3 refers to a unique, definite call to a divine undertaking requiring specialized preparation and deep devotion. Not only is it necessary to determine whether the context is religious or secular in order to understand what is being communicated, but also one must know the specifics of the context. Ambiguity is just as likely when these words are used exclusively in a religious setting. For example, a speaker may mean the third sense of "mission" (life purpose) as he talks to a congregation, but the congregation hear the fourth sense (evangelism and church planting). The speaker wants his hearers to consider God's personal call to participate in redemptive activities wherever they may live and through whatever they do professionally (M3), but they hear that the speaker wants them to become professional evangelists and church planters in a foreign country (M4).

Because hearers have their own hierarchy of meanings for mission, they default to meaning in a particular sense, though someone may use "mission" in an entirely different way. Many evangelicals, for example, often consider M4 and M5 more important so these hearers will automatically hear those meanings. For those less religious, mission will always be M1, or mission may be a distorted caricature of M4, void of any compassion and highly self-serving. The word is a confluence of contested meanings. Stephen Neill's quip, "if everything is mission, nothing is mission," (1959:81) sounds truer today than when first spoken in 1959, and one could say that, "the jungle of *mission* verbiage stands badly in need of some cleaning up" (Macquarrie:316).

Recent History of "Mission"

During the latter half of the twentieth century there were a number of attempts to bring clarity to the term "mission". Scholars during that era frequently made a distinction between the singular form "mission" and the plural "missions." For Lesslie Newbigin, "the entire Church is called to *mission*," but *missions* is reserved for those "activities directed to the task of bringing into existence an authentic witness to Christ in situations where such witness is absent" (1977:216).

For some, the boundary between mission and missions established a line between divine and human activities. *Mission* is divine activity, but *missions* includes human and ecclesial activity. Others offer a specific variation of this distinction through capitalized and lowercase forms of "mission." The capitalized *Mission* refers to divine activity, whereas lowercase *mission* is reserved for human endeavors.

Where does one draw the line between ecclesial and evangelistic activity? If mission refers to God's comprehensive purpose of the whole of creation and all that God has called and sent the church to do in connection with that purpose, both human and divine activity, then mission is everything. Yet whether singular or plural, referring to divine or ecclesial activity, mission is still ambiguous.

These versions of the mission-missions distinction pale in comparison to the use of mission that originates in the twentieth century and is still gaining momentum: that is, the idea of *missio Dei* or the mission of God. In most cases, proponents of the idea of *missio Dei* equate it with the singular form of mission, thereby aiming to distinguish the contemporary practice of mission from that of the eternal mission of the Triune God. For some, *missio Dei* refers to divine essence (this is who God is in himself), and for others it signifies divine operation (this is what God does among humanity). Thus, one could say the who and what of God is *missio Dei* and the who and what of the church is *missio ecclesia*. But by linking God with mission, *missio Dei* appears to be a theological veil, a way to justify talk about ourselves with talk about God.

Furthermore, when we consider how *missio Dei* informs not just our theological concepts but also our practices, it is undeniable that mission remains *missio ecclesia* and church activity morphs into *missio Dei*, which becomes an endorsement for a host of ecclesial endeavors. *Missio Dei* now is the latest branding for a variety of causes and practices, the headliner for youth events and national women conferences, and a way of validating particular strategies.

The stamp of *missio Dei* becomes certainty and proof of divine approval, a wide gate through which almost any concern can pass whether ecclesiology, ecology, ecumenics, liberation or justice. *Missio Dei* is everywhere and means everything.

A more recent addition to the rhetoric of mission has been the introduction of the adjective "missional," popularized by the publication of *The Missional Church* (1998). Rather than speaking of a missionary church or a missionary endeavor, these are now referred to as missional church or missional endeavor. With the neologism of "missional," mission becomes more than evangelism, social action, or foreign enterprise.

Missional transforms mission into a barometer of church health referring to *who* the church is and *what* the church does, becoming the new way of talking about mission in all its forms, *missional* vision, *missional* communities, *missional* language, *missional* era, *missional* trip, and *missional* growth. As such, it is the least helpful of mission-related terms.

The confusion grows even greater with the rhetoric of "missionary." In its modern technical sense, a missionary is an agent sent by an ecclesial or religious body to evangelize others. Yet, for those outside the church, missionary has become synonymous with any fanatical, puritanical, narrow-minded, passionate crusader or bigot. Such a caricature can be seen in contemporary movies and literature, and even in the language of business and politics. When employed as an adjective, missionary modifies all kinds of nouns in order to give these a mission character, hue, or designation. So, calling becomes *missionary* calling, a church is a *missionary* church, work becomes *missionary* work, and lands become *missionary* lands. As an adjective, missionary can modify anything, including secular ideas: the salesman pursues his goals with *missionary* zeal; the missionary fervor of a politician seeking votes. "Missionary" indiscriminately communicates zeal or enthusiasm for any task or cause.

Questioning Mission

For many Christians, mission language is emotionally charged and gives definition to how they feel about their place in the world and how to view those who are different. Yet scholars and practitioners of mission are sounding an alarm, tracing the demise of Western, modern mission, and concluding that it "has lost its credibility and can no longer survive." Lesslie Newbigin contends, "there is need for penitence on the side of 'missions'. The whole modern mission movement is full of the marks of man's greatness and misery." While much good has been accomplished, "the missionary movement of the past two centuries, has been profoundly infected by cultural and economic domination, by paternalism, by all the elements which have brought colonialism into disrepute in so many parts of the world." He goes on to argue that the "traditional picture of the missionary enterprise [...] of the lonely pioneer going out from the secure citadel of Christendom into the world of heathendom [...] must be redrawn, and the way forward for 'missions' must begin with repentance" (1958:14).

Hendrik Kraemer, missionary statesmen of the last century, suggests that the chief problem lies within mission itself. So, rather than rehabilitating or redeeming mission, the task must be substantially more.

In my assessment, it is not that mission *has* a problem, mission *is* the problem. Modern mission is a barrier to faithful witness to Jesus Christ. The solution to the problem does not lie in a simple return to an earlier missionary consciousness and practice. A new vision requires another kind of paradigm shift within the framework of mission. In reality the shift to the rhetoric of mission and missionary in the sixteenth century gave rise and formed what became known as modern mission. This has been the defining shift. And in the early twenty-first century, a second shift is taking place. The more demanding task today calls for us to do more than justify, revise, promote, and bolster mission. Rather, the pioneering task is to acknowledge the habits of language and thought that developed around "mission" beginning in the sixteenth century and to trial new expressions for the church's encounter with the world.

Just as a physician who hears the complaints from a patient with a headache, fever, and neck pain must probe beyond symptoms for the possibility of a more serious condition, our investigation into mission must do more than treat the symptoms of murky or confusing language. We must press beyond symptoms to an examination of the source and suppositions of mission. Thus, what follows in this book is a multifaceted investigation into the language of mission.

My concern is not just to dismiss mission language or to harm the church's witness and service to the world. Nor do I believe it is possible or even wise to abandon mission language altogether. Rather, the aim is to identify the source and severity of the mission problem and offer language that I feel more appropriately expresses the church's being and activity for the time in which we live. The hope is to strengthen and fortify the witness and life of the church, not to minimize or destroy it. My aim is not to denigrate or ridicule the sacrifice and devotion of those who have crossed cultures throughout the years to give witness to Jesus Christ, or to discount the fact that Christianity has expanded throughout the world. However, we no longer live in "the Great Century" of missionary expansion. We live on this side of two World Wars and in the midst of the new realities of increasing pluralism, disintermediated conversations, and localized expressions of faith. Because language frames and represents our understanding of reality, that in turn forms our response to the real world, the way we identify ourselves in the present world situation, and how we act toward others must be carefully considered. Because of the power and effect of mission in its meaning and use, we must probe beyond its surface, do more than rehabilitate it. The hope is to discover fresh impulse and renewed motivation for our witness to the gospel – to transcend mission.

Part I

JUSTIFYING MISSION

1. Partisans and Apologists

> *Christian missions are as old as Christianity itself. The missionary idea, indeed, is much older.*
>
> *Gustav Warneck*

> *Mission is what the Bible is all about; we could as meaningfully talk of the missional basis of the Bible as of the biblical basis of mission.*
>
> *Christopher Wright*

The claims for mission by Gustav Warneck and Christopher Wright are quite grand. Others go further, maintaining that mission stretches back to the beginnings of Christianity and even into divine purposes, while yet others argue that many of the biblical claims for mission are fanciful assertions without a shred of biblical evidence, and they exist only as created myths.

"Mission" and "missionary" are not biblical language but religious terminology, and yet, many within the church assume that both words can be found throughout the pages of the Bible, although the majority of translators throughout the history of the church have not employed either word in their translations of the Old or New Testaments.

Activists and Defenders

Interpreters who endorse the use of mission and missionary can be divided into Partisans and Apologists. Partisans are activists for mission. They read and apply Scripture in order to promote mission endeavors. They proclaim "mission" and "missionary" as biblical without qualifying statements or accompanying evidence leaving the impression that Jesus and Paul speak of "mission" and "missionary," and thus both words are in the Bible to be literally seen and understood. Their concern is to justify missionary work and supply ample motivation for Christians to join the "mission cause." Rarely is the basis from which they make their plea critically examined. This same partisan reading of Scripture can be found among a few within academic circles, where "mission" and "missionary" are often depicted as biblical without critical assessment and argument.

The chief aim of the Partisan is to construct a biblical foundation for both the idea and activity of mission. While this may be viewed as acceptable and necessary, the problem arises when these interpreters assume the meaning of mission as legitimate and coherent, or when scholars fail to acknowledge that "mission" is an interpretative rather than a biblical category. Such an unexamined practice opens the door for Partisans to interpret Scripture from wherever they wish within mission's wide range of meanings or to read into Scripture modern assumptions concerning mission, with a host of fraught assumptions.

Apologists on the other hand recognize the obvious absence of mission in Scripture and seek to establish justification for the term. They address the absence of mission and validate their use of this language by different means.

Biblical Foundation for Mission

The most common method by which Partisans and some Apologists justify mission is through a biblical foundation by collecting texts from here and there, without regard for history and context. Christopher Wright argues that in doing this "we have already decided what we want to prove, that our missionary practice is biblical, and our collection of texts simply ratifies our preconception" (36). But to place, for example, the Abraham narrative alongside other "mission texts" from Scripture disregards the significance of Gen 12:1-3 in the development of Israel's understanding of Yahweh and ignores the richness of the historical setting of the passage. The foundationalist approach accentuates mission at the expense of the historical and contextual phenomena. The result is the neglect and misuse of rich biblical narratives.

Second, a biblical foundation of mission approach is problematic because of its direction. Missionaries and mission promoters tend to read back into the Bible aspects of the missionary enterprise in which they are involved today. In the end, the Bible becomes a utility for mission. Such an approach is not only problematic because it fails to situate the text in relation to its historical contexts, but it also treats the Bible as a source book to justify contemporary mission strategies rather than divine revelation. In order to assert that mission exists in Scripture, one has to locate intents, actions, methods, and structures of mission preaching, mission teams, and missionaries within Scripture. Constructing a basis for mission practices minimizes the Bible as revelation of who God is and as a record of divine activity in the world. The Bible becomes a manual for how to go about a human endeavor. The primary purpose of Scripture is not to provide a foundation for human cause and activity, but to witness to the fact that God often opposes human striving and activity rather than approving them.

In the end, the biblical foundation argument can become a kind of litmus test for who is really Christian or orthodox and who is not. If mission is the core, as old as Scripture, and what the Bible is all about, then it is reasonable to assume that the person or group that is less than enthusiastic about mission is in some measure less committed as a Christian.

Missional Hermeneutic

Many who write about the intersection of mission and Scripture have shifted from a foundationalist approach to reading the Bible with a missional hermeneutic, interpreting the whole of Scripture through the lens of "mission" rather than selected texts. Mission becomes the door of access into Scripture's meaning.

The chief advocates for a missional hermeneutic build their case on a generalized, comprehensive definition of mission. For example, Michael Barram views mission as before and above all else located in the *missio Dei*, and thus, encompasses all of creation and all of God's activity within the created order. Thus, such a hermeneutic is suitable to interpret all of Scripture (42-43, 58). Christopher Wright in a similar manner sees mission simply depicting God as active and purposeful in all history and creation (37). Wright tries to distance this generalized understanding of mission from modern mission and the missionary, and yet divine intention becomes specific missionary actions. In the end, Wright's use of comprehensive, encompassing language of mission conflates divine and human activity.

Given the recent rhetorical history of the language of "mission" that is traced in later chapters, the idea of a missional hermeneutic is yet another modern addition to Christian history and thought. Therefore, the need for a *missional* hermeneutic is questionable, as it represents an imposition of foreign notions on the sacred texts being interpreted.

Christopher Wright insists that rather than creating a bias, "a missional hermeneutic of the whole Bible" subsumes other hermeneutics and offers a way to read the Bible's "coherent story with a universal claim" amidst so many particular stories and claims. Wright argues that mission is uniquely qualified, because it integrates and provides coherence and wholeness to Scripture, allowing the interpreter "to identify some of the underlying themes that are woven all through the Bible's grand narrative" (17-18). Wright's attempt to provide a comprehensive framework to the biblical narrative is certainly worthwhile and needed, and yet, is mission the necessary, or best, "hermeneutical map" for this task?

While far better than a biblical foundation for mission, a missional hermeneutic is suspect in its own way, saying, in effect, "I have a prejudiced starting point. I am reading Scripture from a prior understanding that anticipates a certain outcome." The fact that one admits a hermeneutical starting point does not make that particular hermeneutical approach legitimate. Part of the process of exegesis is to identify and inspect the lenses through which we read the text. While one's own personal bias or prejudice cannot be avoided, the text is paramount and the interpreter should stand before it humbly and pray, that through scholarly methods and questions God's word will be heard afresh. In order to do this, one must admit and avoid biases, not add more.

The chief criticism of a missional hermeneutic is that it qualifies activities, institutions, and attitudes as mission and missionary. Read through the hermeneutical lens of mission, preaching becomes *missionary preaching*, work becomes *missionary work*, method becomes *missionary method*, activity becomes *missionary activity*, and experience becomes *missionary experience*. Once the whole of Scripture passes through the filter of a missional hermeneutic, every piece looks like mission and this leads to distortion. The biblical language of covenant, love, blessing, and election are deemed inadequate, and in need of a qualifying "missional" adjective.

Mission Themes

In an attempt to rescue mission from the tendencies of establishing a biblical foundation or a missional hermeneutic, some have identified missionary themes across Scripture. Through these, interpreters highlight "mission intent" or "mission consciousness" within Scripture, often acknowledging that themes or motifs appear within certain books of the Bible. This approach is quite different from a foundationalist approach, as it offers "mission" as a frame of reference that guides the reading both the Old and New Testaments, but it is only slightly different from a missional hermeneutic. As such, this method is a bit more modest in its claims.

Some claim that the Bible actually begins with the theme of missions in the Book of Genesis and maintains that driving passion throughout the entire Old Testament and on into the New Testament. Others identify the "missionary impulse" or "missionary thrust" in the prophets, Gospels, and Epistles, and read the New Testament with the intent of locating a missionary dimension and intention in all kinds of activity, maintaining that these are true to the "missionary idea," because they are accompanied by "missionary praxis," identified specifically as going and witnessing.

Yet in each of these three methods, whether constructing a foundation, employing a missional hermeneutic, or focusing on mission themes, each dodges the linguistic conflation and the historical contingencies of the language of "mission."

The approach of the Apologists is to trace the route that leads from the biblical languages to the English term "mission." Such a lexical trail begins with the Greek *apostellein* and *pempein*, and then moves to the Latin *missio*, and finally arrives at "mission." The quest is to establish a biblical pedigree for mission through linguistic genealogy. Some create an even longer trail beginning with the Hebrew term *salah* (to send), and then move to Greek, Latin, and the modern equivalent. For these interpreters, mission originates from the Hebrew concept of sending, especially in the divine sending of messengers (prophets and angels). Whether the trail begins with the Hebrew or the Greek, the principal aim is to justify mission by way of its biblical lineage.

One interpreter who justifies mission via a lexical trail is Lucien Cerfaux. He makes the assumption that there is a direct connection between apostolate and missionary, and thus, mission must be the pattern for all people at all times. By extension, he then asserts that Paul is a "missionary" with "missionary destination" and an "apostolic mission" (3). Once a lexical trail is established, the interpreter is able by extension to connect mission language to a host of concepts and ideas. In other words, the effort to link *apostolos* and *apostellein* to mission language does not stop with evidence of a trail but turns into a matter of wider interpretation. Persons, activities, institutions, and locations are designated as "missionary" based on an established trail.

Apostellein, the verb form, is found 135 times in the New Testament and conveys the idea of sending out or sending forth. This verb carries both a general and specified meaning. In its general sense, *apostellein* refers to a wide range of sending of persons and objects: Herod *sends* those who kill male children (Matt 2:16), demons beg to be sent into swine (Matt 8:31), a message or word is *sent* forth (Matt 14:35), and workers are *sent* into the vineyard (Matt 20:2). These instances are ordinary and commonplace kinds of sending.

However, the more prevalent use of *apostellein* refers to the sending of an envoy, ambassador, or representative, and thus, "sending implies a commission bound up with the person of the one sent." In secular Greek, this representative kind of sending is from a monarch, king, or another authority, and thus the sending carries with it deputation. In the New Testament, we see this type of sending applied to a variety of people and situations: the twelve disciples, the seventy-two, the Son, John the Baptist, and many others. In this use, the sending is for a definite purpose or intent, and the one sent thus carries with them authorization of the one who sends. In most New Testament instances of the verb, the authorization or authority is divine in origin and not from another human being.

The noun form *apostole* occurs only four times. Translators have rendered the term with consistency as "apostolate" and "apostolic ministry" or "the ministry which an apostle performs." An apostolate has less to do with an office and more with being charged with a message; in other words, the conveying of this message is the chief function of the apostle.

Apostolos is more frequent (79 times) and specifies one who has been sent, a messenger. The one sent is under assignment to represent another and responsible to the sender. In its primary New Testament use, *apostolos* denotes one who is sent with authority to bear the gospel message, and Christ himself is referred to as *apostolos* (Heb 3:1).

Translators of Greek to Latin and Greek to English rarely render *apostellein*, *apostello*, *apostole*, and *apostolos* as "mission" and "missionary." In Latin translations, *apostolos* has infrequently been translated into corresponding Latin words (*mittere*, *missi*). Instead, the Greek has been used as loan words (e.g. *apostolus*), especially for ecclesiastical references. In the case of Greek to modern English translations and paraphrases versions of Scripture, translators have seldom rendered the Greek as "mission" and "missionary." When they have done so, these are interpretative concepts and not literal translations of the Greek. The claim of lexical trail for "mission" as a biblical word is built on equivalence and not literal translation, and as proof for mission it claims too much.

Second, the lexical trail as an approach falls prey to the "root fallacy." A word may be related semantically or historically but not share the same meaning with the root from which it evolves. In order for mission to be argued from *apostello*, the distinct semantic values of the two words, *apostello* and "mission," must be overlooked. Wholesale translation of *apostello* to "mission" disregards the wide uses, ranging contexts, and variant meanings of the root term. With the lexical trail, the basic assumption made by the Apologist is that in "'sending,' there is the idea of mission," (DuBose:11) and thus, the meaning of mission is within the biblical term and a connection can in most cases, if not always, be inferred and established.

Third, the lexical trail approach underappreciates the extent to which the various forms of *apostellein* and *pempein* differ in use and meaning across the Gospels and Epistles. In the case of *apostello*, in some passages Paul uses the word to refer to authority equal with that of Peter, while elsewhere he uses the word to assert his claim against those who preach another gospel. Each use has a context that should be appreciated and not ignored. When the meaning of a word is transferred from one place to another, the particularity or textual meanings are ignored and often lost. As James Barr notes, problems arise "when the 'meaning' of a word is read into a particular case as its sense and implication there" (218). In the case of mission, even if mission's meaning might be assigned to *apostolos* in one syntactical context, the same meaning does not necessarily transfer to the same word in another.

Fourth, while the linguistic trail purports to demonstrate a link between mission and New Testament words, it is in fact only a third-hand etymological connection. The English word mission is not the

Greek word *apostello*, and missionary is not *apostolos*. In order to connect mission and apostle, the interpreter must turn to Latin, not Greek. Apologists assert that mission and missionary have their roots in the Latin word *mittere*, meaning to send, and they are correct. Mission is the English translation of *mittere*. And yet, while *mittere* is the Latin translation of *apostello* and mission is the English translation of *mittere*, there is not necessarily a trail of meaning from *apostello* to *mittere* to mission. Equality of meaning is assumed, because there is similarity in form, sound, and spelling. And yet, though the modern English word looks and sounds like the Latin *mittere* or *missio*, there is a difference in meaning.

The leap from *mittere* to mission was not made in any of the Latin or early English translations. Though the Latin Vulgate renders the Greek verbs *apostellein* and *pempein* as *mittere*, the trail stops there. The noun form, *apostolos*, was considered unique enough that Jerome and those who followed him transliterated it rather than use a Latin equivalence. The nouns *missionibus* and *missionarius* are nowhere to be found in the Latin Vulgate. And the earliest English translations of the Vulgate do not turn *mittere* into "mission" or "missionary." It is only in the modern era that a connection between *mittere* and "mission" is made and only with Apologists does the lexical trail appear. A leap from what was originally meant and preserved in the text as *apostellein*, *apostolos*, and *apostole*, to the modern expressions of mission, disregards the fact that translators did not acknowledge the connection, nor did they create a trail. Instead, the lexical trail too easily traces mission from English to Latin to Greek and back again from Greek to Latin to English. By this means of justifying mission, the interpreter disregards the translator, and the translator disagrees with the interpreter.

In the end, justifying mission by means of a linguistic trail is faulty. The alleged trail from biblical words to mission can only be inferred and not literally established. And yet, the greater issue is that a quest to justify mission through "sending" terms impoverishes one's interpretation of Scripture and denies other important emphases their place. To base one's argument on a single Greek word and its Latin equivalence, *mittere*, accentuates "sending" over all other dimensions of redemptive history and activity. The mission tail ends up wagging the whole dog. Because of these difficulties, Apologists have shifted away from trying to establish a direct lexical trail from biblical words to mission and moved to a broader, more encompassing means of establishing mission in terms of a semantic field.

A semantic domain or field is a linguistic range that represents an idea or concept. Semantic field theory operates on the assumption that related words, though not synonymous, taken together refer to a general phenomenon. Words and phrases find common meaning and are thus members of a class. For example, bluebonnets and roses are flowers. Flower is the category under which bluebonnets and roses can be grouped. Bluebonnets and roses are in the field of flowers (literally and figuratively). In the same way, Apologists justify mission with the claim that certain activities, people, places, and goals belong to the semantic field of "mission." Because these are members of the class called mission, and thus related to mission, they, in turn, are able to substantiate mission.

Thus in order to identify words and phrases belonging to semantic domains related to mission, a working definition of mission is first established. This definition then provides a basis for establishing the semantic field. Once the field is populated, the definition is revisited and measured against the semantic field. Mission justifies "mission." In both the initial and revisited definitions, mission is assumed and not questioned. In other words, a definition of the term is formed as a basis for the semantic field and mission justified by the field without questioning mission, its source, meaning, and assumptions. Both the terminology of mission and the field of mission are assumed, and thus an *a priori* definition based on contemporary notions of mission commands the field. The argument is tautological.

The chief problem in this method of justifying "mission" is the amalgamation of meanings. When lumped together under one class, differences of meaning in the various words and phrases are compromised. In the end such an amalgamation spreads the meaning of mission across a wide range of words, and mission becomes an all-inclusive category for all manner of ideas to be associated with it. The circularity of this process highlights what little foundation is necessary to construct a theology of mission. Apologists take the general and inclusive concept, "mission," and translate it into definite events and actions. "Mission" describes and justifies mission.

The difficulty with all of these methods is in where they begin. Rather than arguing from Scripture to mission, the rhetoric of mission frames the linguistic starting point. Partisans and Apologists build a biblical foundation for mission, read Scripture through a mission hermeneutic, and look for themes with mission as the beginning point. Either way, this kind of justification represents a herculean effort to establish a case for the term while obscuring or ignoring historical and textual meaning.

Thus, Partisans read mission into Scripture without qualification or explanation while Apologists recognize the absence of mission and missionary in the biblical text and devise ways to construct links to mission-language by means of a lexical trail. For both, their aim is to justify mission. Once justified, the task is to interpret Scripture in light of mission, and to construct a mission theology which mobilizes personnel and resources. The end result is that as a supplied word, mission dominates the reading of Scripture.

2. Reading Scripture as Mission

Here we are confronted with the real starting point of the primitive Christian mission: it lies in the conduct of Jesus himself. If anyone is to be called "the primal missionary," he must be.

Martin Hengel

Two questions need to be raised regarding Scripture and mission: To what extent is "mission interpretation" used to read Scripture? What difficulty does this kind of interpretation pose?

Old Testament and Mission

Only a minority of interpreters explore mission as a theme in the Old Testament. There are those who say mission is completely absent for Israel, and it is not found in the Old Testament (Bosch:17). They maintain that if mission is to be found in Scripture it begins only with Jesus and the early church and that while Israel may have believed in the universal nature of its religion and sensed the need to make God known among the other nations, signs of Israel moving toward the nations to convert others to the worship of God are absent.

Christopher Wright takes a mediating view as he defines mission in the more general sense of a long-term purpose or goal, and thus he feels at liberty to use mission language throughout his Old Testament discussion. Where he draws the line is with the word "missionary," since Israel was not mandated by God to send missionaries to the nations, nor were they condemned for their failure to play a missionary role among the nations. Wright affirms "mission" as God's general purpose in the Old Testament but does not find sending and evangelization by Israel, as these connote missionary kinds of activities (23, 24). And yet he encourages the reader to connect their treatment of mission in the Old Testament to contemporary missionary efforts. He also connects his specialized, Old Testament use of mission with familiar New Testament uses of mission: the early Christian mission, the Gentile mission, the missionary task, Paul's missionary journeys, and the "missionary apostles" (502-03).

On the other hand, some see mission and missionaries throughout the Old Testament, with the Old Testament themes of universalism and covenant, asserting that Israel was to be God's missionaries to the world, calling Psalm 67 "a missionary psalm," and insisting that the whole Bible offers a "missionary vision." They identify the Servant figure in Isaiah as "a missionary servant," characterizing Israel's call as "an active missionary call," and argue that Jonah is "a missionary book" (Glover:15, 17; Kaiser:20, 60). Others describe Abraham as one of a number of Old Testament characters who were striking examples of missionary spirit and effort, along with Joseph, Moses, and Jonah, and argue that the book of Esther is a fascinating missionary narrative as well as a thrilling missionary romance (Glover:17-20).

H. H. Rowley insists that "the Old Testament is a missionary book," and yet he concedes this is not because Israel saw itself as a people of missionaries but because the monotheistic faith of Israel must include a vision of nations worshipping Yahweh (76-77). The overall intent is that Yahweh be known not just in Israel or only among a particular people but among all the peoples of the earth. Universal regard for the nations and divine activity toward them are identified as "mission."

Yet critics note that even a cursory reading of the Old Testament shows that Israel does not view itself as the agent of mission, and while the nations are part of the Old Testament story and there is divine regard for them, God's intention is expressed in the language of love, covenant, and election, but not mission.

Then there are those who see mission as an Old Testament theological category, which contains theological expressions or models of mission expressed in election and covenant, divine actions of God who is a missionary God. Critics of this third position do so either on the basis of a narrow definition of mission (i.e. as only the sending of human agents), or because mission-language terms are too limiting to describe God. For them, mission must involve human agents who believe in God's universality and thus actively bring non-believers into the knowledge and worship of God. To employ mission strictly as a theological term is too all-encompassing or indefinite, and thus not real mission. For others, to ascribe to God such a human attribute as "mission" and "missionary" restricts the transcendent nature of the divine. In either case, the problem is that too little or too much is made of mission. Difficulty lies in the imprecise nature of the language of mission itself.

In these approaches, the manner in which mission is defined and used determines one's interpretation of the Old Testament. To define mission as a human agency restricts its use to what Israel does in response to interactions with peoples surrounding them. Framing one's interpretation within this definition creates the expectation that Israel is to look and act like contemporary expressions of mission and missionary. By such standards, Israel certainly fails to look missionary. The rhetoric of mission unfairly condemns Israel.

On the other hand, if one's definition includes all of the activity of God, then mission is a transcendent reality. Mission becomes everything. If the aim is to speak inclusively of God and his activities, covenant, love, and reconciliation are much better words.

New Testament and Mission

Interpreters often describe the New Testament as a mission story from beginning to end because, "Jesus himself is on a mission and because the story ends with Jesus sending his followers on a mission to the nations" (Williams:50). Interpreters point to the predominance of sending in the Gospels, Acts, and the Epistles as evidence of the mission-nature of the New Testament, and thus describe the letters of the New Testament as "missionary documents written in the context of missionary advance" (Pratt, Still, Walters:22-26). As stated in the previous chapter, the idea of sending, expressed in the two verbs *pempein* and *apostellein*, forms the primary argument for these claims.

In the mission approach to the New Testament, interpreters use mission as a noun to designate institution, movement, and collective action, and as an adjective to qualify various nouns. Interpreters make reference to "the early Christian mission," "Judean mission," "Gentile mission," "Samaritan mission," and so forth. As a noun, mission identifies specific ideas, actions, and people, and it conveys the idea of task, assignment, or organized work that is definitive and historical. The "Samaritan mission," for example, refers to specific actions by Jesus at a particular place and time in history, yet there was no such thing as *the* Samaritan mission, as if such a program was the intent of Jesus or the disciples. Rather than the segregation of places, peoples, or times into definitive missions, we read of Jesus crossing social and religious boundaries in every direction at the same time without special descriptors.

In addition, New Testament interpreters frequently use "missionary" as an adjective to qualify concepts and activities, referring to *missionary* activity, *missionary* practices, *missionary* work, and in many other ways. Thus rather than just traveling, the trip is a *missionary* trip. Rather than proclaiming a message, the message being proclaimed is a *missionary* message. The criteria for designating these concepts and activities as "mission" or "missionary" are unstated and appear to be arbitrary, which limits the scope and intent of preaching, travels, discourse, and work to an ambiguous and unwieldly category.

Likewise, named individuals and groups of people are given the title of "missionary," designating a role for a person doing a specific task or job. Interpreters replace names, such as Mark, John, Matthew, Aquila, Priscilla, Timothy, and others, with the designation of "missionary" in order to depict their actions as particularly related to mission. In so doing, they give the impression that these individuals and groups of people have a designated task or a vocational and professional designation. Such replacement represents either a high degree of interpretation or blatant suppositions about profession placed onto first-century men and women. Mark does not describe himself as a "missionary," and he performs a variety of activities, none of which he designates as "mission." The disciples' aims, intents, activities, and identities are much larger than what might be conveyed in the term "missionary."

It is confusing to convey the notion that actors in the early church or those who wrote the New Testament documents had a "missiology." While the intent may be to say Mark and Matthew were thoughtful as they acted, they could not have had a missiology, since the academic study of mission was not established until the nineteenth century. To characterize their thought as missiology is saying too much and, first and foremost, they were mere witnesses, offering an account of what they had witnessed of Jesus' life, death, and resurrection.

Jesus and Mission

Some suggest that while mission might be questionable in other parts of Scripture, the assumption is that mission is at the heart of what Jesus said and did. And yet, while a myriad of Jesus' words, images, and directives point to witness, proclamation, and love, "mission" is not recorded as among the utterances of Jesus or registered as his intent.

The contention is that just as Jesus is sent from the Father, so the early disciples and church are sent. The Father sends Jesus, and Jesus sends his disciples in the same way. But equating Jesus' "sentness" and mission presents several difficulties. First, Jesus refers to sending, not mission. A plain statement is transformed into a complex concept of strategy, organization, and profession. Once a leap is made from sending to mission, the horizon of the present eclipses that of the text.

Second, in such an interpretation, mission overwhelms and then monopolies other themes and emphases in Jesus' words. In an effort to justify mission as a concept, the richness of the incarnation is minimized, consigning divine sending to human mission, and divine intent to missionary vocation.

Third, Jesus' emphasis is on something beyond the operation of sending, more than the pursuit of "mission." After his resurrection Jesus focuses his disciples' attention on his hands and side, on his wounds. He then says, "Peace be with you, as the Father has sent me, I also send you" (Jn 20:21). Once again, sending is a modest means to the grand goal of redemption. When conveyance to this end becomes the emphasis rather than the end itself, the implications of Jesus' death and his victory over sin lose their place of importance.

What we find in Scripture is that those whom Jesus calls are given a variety of titles. They are named as apostles, disciples, and the Twelve, but not "missionaries." In parallel passages, "apostle" is used in place of "disciple." Thus, not even *apostle* is a fixed title for a vocation or a designation for a particular group of people; rather, it is a descriptive term to denote that the disciples are among those who are sent. Yet, interpreters portray "missionary" as a fixed title and as an established vocation.

It has been argued that Jesus' call to the disciples to be "fishers of people" (Mark 1:16-30) entails something other than obedience (follow me) and action (fish for people), and that their vocation after this call became missionary, but this is untenable. First, the text does not state this as the case. Second, this interpretation forces Jesus' calling of these fishermen into a specialized and modern notion of vocation (profession and missionary). On the other hand, to read this text as a summons to be a disciple who simply "fishes for people" opens the possibility for people of all kinds of abilities and vocational callings to participate in fishing for people. To read profession into the text limits "fishing" to people who are professionals and construes Jesus' summons in the terms of a profession.

Others point to the universal dimension in Jesus' self-designation, "Son of Man," as indication of his mission self-understanding. But, once again, must the universality of "Son of Man" mean "mission"? Such interpretations of Jesus and mission set the stage to view Paul and the early church as fully vested in "mission," complete with missionaries and mission strategies. With the mission premise in place, the step from Jesus the missionary to Paul the missionary is an easy one.

Paul the Missionary

For many people, the apostle Paul embodies what we mean by "missionary." The majority of interpreters simply characterize Paul as "a missionary" or add qualifying adjectives: such as "the greatest missionary of history." Paul the Apostle and Paul the missionary are synonymous. The argument moves in a circular fashion: mission identifies Paul, Paul defines mission.

However, Paul identifies himself not as a missionary but as an apostle, one who is sent. His self-designation of *apostle* is often offered as firm evidence that Paul understood himself as a missionary, but a careful reading of various texts shows Paul's use of apostle can be interpreted in a number of ways. The term embodies his appeal to authority, as well as responsibility, as he writes to churches to instruct them in matters of practice, and the term is even used over against those who preach a different gospel (1 Cor 9:1-2). In some instances, he uses the term to assert his authority in matters of belief and practice among the churches. When Paul identifies himself, it is not as a missionary, but as an apostle, a bond servant, a prisoner of Christ Jesus, and an ambassador. No one title or designation is definitive. Paul continued as a leatherworker and supported himself, and did not become a full-time professional of any kind. He proclaimed the name of Christ to everyone he encountered, never in the name of mission or under the identity of missionary.

Because Paul is assumed to be a missionary, those who accompanied him are seen as missionaries and part of his missionary team. But to characterize Paul as having a "missionary organization," presents an erroneous picture of the nature and scope of his work and those who labored with him. In addition to those on the "mission team," others are characterized as "mission supporters," sympathizers who stood with Paul, convinced of his cause and the validity of his apostleship. And yet, the effect is that through such language Paul and his band are subtly transformed into a modern mission team, with accompanying modern assumptions about organization, supporters, and finances.

The intent in many cases seems to be to prove that Paul had a particular strategy and methodology, and then maintain that these strategies and methods are the ones modern missionaries should employ, but it does not appear that Paul differentiates between methods that are missionary and those that are non-missionary.

John Townsend maintains that the designation of missionary journeys was imposed on Acts with the rise of Catholic and Protestant mission societies (103). He traces the earliest reference to "missionary journey" language to J. A. Bengel's *Gnomon Novi Testamenti* (1742). Evidence of this influence can be seen in the language of "missionary journey" that has been inserted as subject headings in modern translations of Acts.

The recurring refrain of "Paul's mission" fills the pages of commentaries and textbooks. It is "Paul's missionary thrust into the Greco-Roman world," and his "missionary responsibility" (Barnett:6). The result is that "mission" becomes defined as originating from Paul and belonging to Paul. Mission defines Paul, as he is made into the mission prototype, strategist, and hero.

Early Church

Even as Paul becomes the founder of a "missionary church," commentators on the book of Acts and early Christianity reflect this history through the paradigm of our modern missionary language. Much has been made of how the early church was "a genuinely missionary church," with "missionary spirit," "missionary zeal," and "missionary work," operating according to "missionary principles." Such sweeping characterizations often eclipse the other realities of the early church, such as its struggle with race, order, and false teachings. It was also known to have bouts of division, laxness, and immorality. And yet, attempts are frequently made to paint a picture of the nascent church solely as a *missionary* entity or as embodying the *mission* ideal. This not only inflates one dimension but also anachronistically misrepresents much that transpires in the early years following Christ. Far from a pristine, mono-dimensional exemplar of mission, the early church, much like the church today, struggled with its own identity and purpose.

The concepts of "mission" and "missionary" are not developed in the book of Acts, nor do they exist as terminology or ideals toward which the early church aspired. This language distorts the story implying that being the church was not enough. A church had to be or should be a "missionary" church. Yet saints at Ephesus and Galatia are known to Paul simply as "church."

Paul writes against converts or churches belonging to himself or anyone else and speaks of these churches as having all they need to be the church in their cities and provinces. They are simple known as *ecclesia*, or assemblies of new believers, and the primary actor in the Book of Acts is the Holy Spirit and not a church "deeply imbued with the missionary spirit" (Glover:39).

Profane and Sacred Language

When "mission" is exalted to the status of a biblical word as a means for justifying contemporary paradigms and programs, it diminishes the place of more theologically rich and biblical concepts, such as covenant, reconciliation, witness, and love. The great themes of

Scripture become lost or obscure when "mission" and "missionary" control the text. Scripture becomes a means to justify mission.

3. Presenting History as Mission

He admonishes and teaches, saying,
Going therefore teach now all the gentiles,
Baptizing them in the name of the Father and the Son and the Holy Spirit,
teaching them to observe all things whatsoever I have commanded to you,
and look, I am with you all days,
as far as the highest perfection of the age.
And again He says, Going therefore into the entire world,
Proclaim the Gospel to every creature.

Patrick

Various words have been used throughout history to explain the expansion of Christianity, and mission has not always been the word of choice. It is absent from the language used by its earliest historians. Patrick and The Venerable Bede tell this story in language quite different from that of modern mission historians. Instead of "mission," these early historians employ the language of *witness*, *pilgrimage*, and *martyrdom*. Rather than "missionaries," they name the actors as *bishops*, *pilgrims*, *servants*, and *apostles*.

The story of ***Patrick*** (c. 385-460) is linked to the arrival of Christianity in Ireland. The facts of his life are sparse and the accounts of his activities vary widely. Stories of his birth, life at home, years as a slave, return to Britain, and his activities in Ireland are considered to be equal parts hagiography and history. The earliest histories of Patrick's life, such as Muirchú moccu Macthéni's *Vita Patricii* (*Life of Patrick*), composed in the seventh century, must not be read as critical or exacting histories that provide precise accounts of what did and did not happen. Rather, their purpose is to provide a sympathetic remembrance of Patrick during his lifetime and a commemoration of the beginning of Irish Christianity.

Muirchú, in *Vita Patricii*, uses a variety of designations to refer to Patrick as confessor, holy man, saint, bishop, eminent teacher, Christian, and apostolic man. According to Muirchú, Patrick is like Jonah, Moses, John the Baptist, and Paul, and is compared to Gideon, Stephen, and Christ. Muirchú reports Patrick's involvement in a number of activities, including preaching and teaching. And in one instance, an old friend, Victoricus, tells Patrick that it is "time for him to fish with the evangelical net among the wild and barbarian nations" (9). In addition to baptizing, teaching, and converting, Muirchú reports that Patrick performs miracles and raises the dead. *Epistola ad milites Corotici* is Patrick's fierce condemnation of a British warrior named Coroticus where the language he uses most to describe his sojourn in Ireland is pilgrimage.

Nowhere do we find the intent expressed by Patrick or those who record his life to name him as a "missionary" or associate him with "mission." And yet, contrary to Patrick and Muirchú, modern historians name Patrick as "the missionary from Roman Britain," "the first great missionary to Ireland," and "a model for foreign missionaries," and depict his return to Ireland as a "mission" or as "missionary labour."

The way in which historians use the language of mission to describe Patrick varies. If commissioned by Rome, then Patrick was a missionary, and yet, the writings of St. Patrick himself contain not the remotest hint of such a mission. F. F. Bruce describes Patrick's encounters with social structures and political figures as "missionary campaigns" (378). But "mission" is not the language of Patrick or his contemporaries, but an anachronistic imposition which repositions and repurposes Patrick, transporting Patrick from the fifth century into the modern era, altering not only the story but the person.

The same is true of ***Columba*** (c. 520-597) who lands on Iona in 563 and establishes a monastery on the island. St. Adomanán, ninth abbot at Iona from 679 to 704, wrote *Vita Columbae* (*Life of St Columba*) approximately a century after Columba's death. According to Adomanán, "Columba sailed away from Ireland to Britain, choosing to be a pilgrim for Christ" (105). Columba is not sent on a "mission" and the missionary life is never mentioned as his motivation, task, or vocation. In the same way, The Venerable Bede's *Ecclesiastical History of the English People*, does not identify Columba as a "missionary" or his activity as "mission."

Yet modern historians often characterize Columba's move to Iona as a "mission," name him a "missionary," and portray the monastery at Iona as a "headquarters for a major missionary movement." Such designations and descriptions suggest intentions and plans that

Columba himself does not claim and that his contemporaries do not attribute to him.

The same can be argued for ***Columban*** (c. 543-615), another Irish monk, who travels from the monastery of Bangor with twelve others to Brittany in eastern France where the group establishes a monastery at Luxeuil. Though named as a "missionary" by both popular and scholarly historians, Columban only self-describes as a *monk* and a *pilgrim*.

Both Columba and Columban operated out of the Irish tradition of *peregrine* (wandering) and thus were *peregrinatio pro Christo* (wandering for the sake of Christ). Pilgrim-monks roamed as an act of love for God and to express their devotion by way of exile from home and kin. Their purpose was not overt evangelization, rather the faith went with them as they established outposts for Christianity in the places to which they went. They did not always travel among pagans but often among peoples who were already Christianized or those in the process of being brought into the sphere of the Roman Church, its ecclesiastical structures and hierarchy. Thus, they did not set out on pilgrimage with the expressed purpose of spreading Christianity to new areas. Pilgrimage "was a form of asceticism, not a technique of conversion or evangelical persuasion" (Markus:132). To frame *peregrine* as missionary in intention is to misrepresent the original motivation and aim of pilgrimages.

Gregory I, or ***Gregory the Great*** (590-604) is lauded as the greatest pope of the Middle Ages, whose tenure was marked by extensive reforms within the church and the extension of the Roman Church into England. As pontiff, he sent forty monks to England under the leadership of Augustine to establish the Catholic faith among the

Anglo-Saxons. Initially fearful, Augustine become courageous once he discovers an Anglo-Saxon Christian queen and a bishop. With the queen's help, Augustine is able to speak to King Ethelbert and the king is converted and baptized in 597, and thus Roman Christianity takes root in England. Augustine becomes archbishop of the English people and Canterbury is established as the seat of the episcopal see. Ethelbert does not force his subjects to receive baptism but most follow in their king's decision and become Christians.

As with Patrick, Columba, and Columban, Gregory's initiative and Augustine's endeavors are saturated with mission language. Kenneth Latourette renders the papal initiative of Gregory as the "Roman mission," and those sent by Gregory as "bands of missionaries" (2.72). F. F. Bruce refers to Augustine and companions as a "missionary party" and their work as "missionary operations" (397, 398). Numerous historians proclaim Gregory the Great as the first missionary pope, identify missionary work as his chief accomplishment, and classify efforts toward the Anglo-Saxons as "the Gregorian mission."

And yet, one searches without success in the three volumes of *The Letters of Gregory the Great* to find language that names the extension and establishment of the Roman Church as "mission." Gregory instead refers to himself as a servant of God and uses the language of preaching, teaching, loving neighbors, doing good works, and performing acts of charity. He exhorts others to preach, "bring foreigners to God," "lead pagans to faith," and work toward "the winning of souls" (1.176, 179, 307; 2.307, 354). Those he addresses directly or names in his letters are identified as priests, monks, evangelists, abbesses, nuns, messengers, chaplains, clerics, emissaries, patriarchs, abbots, deacons, and sub-deacons. None of these he addresses or those he writes about are given a missionary classification. In his correspondence soliciting support for the conversion of England to the Catholic faith, Gregory describes Augustine as a "monk" and "bishop," never a "missionary." Likewise, Augustine's task is depicted in numerous ways but not as *missio* or "mission." Rather than lauding Augustine's efforts as a "missionary triumph," Gregory cautions the bishop and his company of monks that "a weak mind puffs itself up in its pride" and "vainglory," and thus brands them as "weak preachers" (2:438-40).

Bede's *Ecclesiastical History* is the most reliable and nearest source to Gregory. Bede calls Gregory the "apostle to the British people" and gives him the title of "a servant of God" who came "to preach the word of God to the English race" (69, 123). Bede notes the significance of the conversion of Ethelbert by Augustine but does not mark this as the start of a "Roman mission." Thus, much like Gregory's own letters, Bede's account suggests that the initiatives of Gregory and Augustine signal the beginning of the Roman Church in the British Isles. The language of the primary actors and chroniclers frames the story as one of papal authority, political conversion, monastic duties, and Catholic dominance, dynamics which become skewed, neglected or lost when cast in the language of mission.

The same can be said of ***Winfrid of Crediton*** or ***Boniface*** (c. 675-754) who is linked to the evangelization of Germany and is best known for confronting pagan practices by felling the Oak of Thor (or Jupiter). Stephen Neill calls him "the greatest of all the missionaries of the Dark Ages" (1986:64), and named by Latourette as "the most famous English missionary to the Continent" (2.85). Yet, because

Boniface is interpreted through the language of "mission" and "missionary," he looks and acts more like a modern professional than a man of the seventh century. For many, Boniface is the mission link between the early church and the modern era. But he is a *missionary* because of what interpreters deem as mission. Instead, bishops, monks, abbesses, kings, and queens address Boniface as a servant of God, beloved brother, fellow-priest, prophet, evangelist, archbishop, father, friend, and martyr, and describe his task chiefly as preaching. Boniface describes himself only as "servant of the servants of God" and bishop.

Willibald, an Anglo-Saxon who wrote an account of Boniface's life within a few years of the saint's death, quotes Boniface as describing himself as an "ambassador of the apostolic see to the western lands of the barbarians," and describes his life as a "long pilgrim journey" or "pilgrimage." While some of Boniface's activity may resonate with our own language of mission, it is mistaken to equate the two.

The ***Nestorians*** are often cited as early missionaries to the East. Described as the most remarkable and far-reaching missionary expansion to China, Alopen and those accompanying him from Persia and Syria, according many commentators, are "Christian missionaries" and their venture is named as "the Christian mission to China" (Foster:43, 44, 47). And yet, earliest records of the Nestorian work in the East do not contain mission language and do not report these efforts as "mission" nor are Nestorians identified as "missionaries." The most substantial evidence of Nestorian presence and activity in China is a black limestone stele erected in 781, known as the Nestorian Monument, and visible today in Xian. It records the arrival of "a Bishop (Lofty Virtue) named Alopen."

Among his activities, "he conveyed the true Scriptures," "he rode through hardship and danger," and brought "[S]criptures and images from afar." The Persians and Syrians listed on the monument are not identified as "missionaries." Instead, they are called priests, monks, archdeacons, and elders. Lost in the mission language are the controversies over the nature of Christ, distinct cultural expressions of Nestorian faith, and motivations behind their far-ranging ventures to the East. Mission language obscures the history and nature of the Nestorian venture into China.

Mission Histories?

Other prominent historians of the early church are evidence of the absence of the terms missionary and mission: Eusebius, Rufinus of Aquileia, Prosper of Aquitaine, and the Venerable Bede. These historians and their histories are of interest for a number of reasons, not least of which because they are often cited in making the historical case for mission. Two of these will be discussed in further detail.

Eusebius of Caesarea (c. 260-339) is best known for *The History of the Church from Christ to Constantine*. Divided into ten books, this chronicles the transition of the church from an outlawed persecuted community to the church at peace and the establishment of Christianity as the religion of the Roman Empire. Eusebius takes in a wide range of themes: the story of Christ, the fate of the Jews, pagan attacks on the faith, martyrdom, episcopal succession, and the writings of the faithful. In his pursuit of these subjects, he refers to prominent individuals, quotes from their sermons and letters, and provides commentary on events within the early church. Eusebius describes the expansion of Christianity as occurring through a range of activities and events: preaching, teaching, evangelizing, sending, spreading the message, sowing of seed, confessing, witnessing, miracles, and martyrdom. He gives the actors in these activities a variety of titles: apostles, bishops, disciples, evangelists, martyrs, preachers, witnesses, fellow-soldiers, ambassadors, and Christians, but never mission or missionary.

When interpreters and translators read mission into Eusebius, two problems surface. First, there is the problem of presumption. "Mission" and "missionary" are presumed as ancient rhetoric and in use during the time of Eusebius, and thus the events and agents of his account are interpreted as referring to an enterprise called "mission." Presumption leads to the establishment of false facts.

The second problem is one of translation. Modern translators of Eusebius insert the language of mission and missionary into the text, when it is not there. The reader then assumes that Greek equivalents of "mission" and "missionary" are Eusebius' actual words. Preference for mission language is especially pronounced in G. A. Williamson's 1965 translation of *History of the Church*. In four places Williamson calls Eusebius' references to Christ's earthly life and endeavors as "His mission" (61, 69, 132). Each of these accounts could be as easily translated with the language of purpose, aim, or intent, but Williamson chooses the imprecise and historically conditioned language of mission. Kirsopp Lake's 1926 translation, on the other hand, offers a more descriptive translation of Christ's activity as preaching and teaching. Once mission and missionary are related as Eusebius' words, they become historical fact, and incorporated into the tradition of earliest Christianity. Eusebius is far too important a source for our understanding of the early church to be handled carelessly, and thus every measure should be made to clarify his meaning. Such measures guard against a misuse of Eusebius and his text and a misreading of the history of the early church.

The Venerable Bede (673-735) writes *Ecclesiastical History of England* (731) to detail the coming of the Christian faith to the British Isles. His account is chiefly the story of the expansion of the Roman Church via Canterbury and the establishment of bishops and monasteries throughout Britain, Scotland, and Ireland. Bede calls the actors in this story bishops, monks, hermits, abbots, priests, pastors, ministers, teachers, confessors, heralds, and martyrs, and characterizes their actions in the establishment of Christianity as preaching, suffering, miracles, evangelistic work, instruction, and righteous living. The aims of these actors and activities, as chronicled by Bede, are the conversion of kings and queens, the building of churches, and the normalization of ecclesiastical structures and practices. Missionaries are not named as actors, and mission is not identified as the means to accomplish these aims. And yet, historians cite mission as Bede's organizing principle and his history as "missionary history," with the "mission of Palladius to the Irish," "the mission of Augustine," and "mission to the Frisians and Saxons" to substantiate the claim that Bede's *Ecclesiastical History* has a "missionary message" (Wood:26, 42, 43, 45). Though many historians treat Bede's *Ecclesiastical History* as mission history with a missionary message, Bede does not use the language of mission or missionary. Bede's Latin is *apostolico* and not *missio*. Mission would infuse Bede's motives incorrectly with modern aims and activities.

Another example is the oft-repeated incident recorded by Bede in which Gregory the Great, before becoming pope, encounters young boys from Britain for sale in a Roman market. He approaches the bishop of Rome and asks him to send "ministers of the word to the Angles in Britain to convert them to Christ." Bede records that Gregory would go himself, but he is unable because of duties in Rome. The Oxford 1969 English translation reports Bede's words as "he was unable to perform this mission." In the Latin text, Bede uses the verb *mitteret*, denoting action rather than a noun. The verb denotes the simple action of sending instead of a formal, planned, or organized mission or even of a general task or purpose. Rendering the verb as a noun and thus turning action into a planned affair or an organized delegation is less than accurate.

Besides the common use of the Latin verb "to send," Bede does use the noun form of *missus* three times. The 1969 Oxford translation consistently renders these as mission whereas earlier translations do not. In one instance, the Oxford translation renders Bede's reference to a priest by the name of Peter, the first abbot of the monastery at Canterbury, as being sent as "a mission to Gaul" (*Galliam missus*). In earlier translations, Peter is named as an emissary for political representation of the church, as there appears to be no intent to evangelize. The Latin text of the Venerable Bede's early history of the expansion of Christianity into England does not preference mission or missionary. The presence of *missus* language in Bede evidences its early use in a diplomatic or representative sense but not as language of the modern mission enterprise.

Thus a careful inspection of the language of historical figures and early historians of the church reveals that "missionary" – as an ecclesiastical title, vocational class, or professional – is non-existent. Those who spread the faith are identified as bishops, disciples, saints, monks, nuns, pilgrims, and martyrs. The closest description that approximates to mission or missionary is "apostolic," but in these cases, the reference is to the office or role similar to that of the twelve disciples and not to a modern vocation.

Interpreters claim that historical figures are talking and writing about "mission," even if these words are not used. And yet, this is precisely the problem. Mission and missionary are unknown concepts to Patrick and Eusebius, and thus, it can only be mission and missionary as modern historians conceive these ideas that are read into their ancient worlds.

While mission classification may seem to be appropriate and helpful, renaming preaching, witnessing, evangelizing, and traveling as "mission" alters reality. Identifying preachers, witnesses, and martyrs as "missionaries" skews identity. The intent of historians is to harmonize different kinds of forms and actors into one reality, but this kind of compression into mission, a single reality, can lead to erroneous conclusions.

4. Rhetoric and Trope

> *The conversion of Britain, as we have indicated, proceeded chiefly from two sources. One was Rome. From this centre of the Western Church, on the initiative of Gregory the Great, came small bands of missionaries.*
>
> *Kenneth Latourette*

According to Kenneth Latourette, Stephen C. Neill, and many other historians, the expansion of Christianity from Jerusalem to the ends of the earth is the story of mission, and thus Christian history is presented *as* mission history. On the other hand, there are some who recount the history of early Christianity with little or no mention of "mission." Their story is told in a manner without reference to mission activities or mission agents. According to these histories, the death and resurrection of Jesus propelled groups of people throughout Palestine speaking of Jesus' life and teaching, death and resurrection, speaking of their experience in the "Jesus Way" Christianity spreads, and yet, mission is not identified as the cause nor are missionaries named as its agents. For them, Christian history is the history of the faith and the church.

The new faith made its way through families, associations, clans, and societies. The "Jesus Way" crossed the boundaries of custom, ethnicity, religion, and language. The astounding effect was that within a few centuries the story based in the teachings and person of Jesus became the faith of Western civilization. Historians describe this progression with many different words apart from mission and while one person or group may prefer one description over another, no one word is definitive or sacred.

Constructing History

The historian selects small fragments from the whole and the reader never receives history as raw data but as selected facts and as an orchestrated interpretation of speculation or conjecture. This is especially true, for example, when a person from Scotland writes a history of India, or an American writes a history of Japan. The limitations of the historian's time and place, language and culture, are compounded by the fact that every historian has a belief structure, a scaffold upon which they determine why causes have certain effects, what motivates people to act, and how systems function.

So, reading history is as much about reading the historian as the actual events. The historian by necessity constructs history based on what they believe happened and what they happen to believe. "Mission" is not just fact or event but one belief structure among many possible structures that governs how a historian might construct history.

History Obscured

Clarity and accuracy in written history are hard enough to achieve without mission language adding its assumptions and aims. It is the rare historian who acknowledges the problem of mission language and thus qualifies his or her use of mission and missionary. Ian Wood, *The Missionary Life: Saints and the Evangelisation of Europe, 400-1050*, uses the language of mission and missionary throughout his discussion only to admit in his conclusion that "there is no classical or medieval Latin word *missionarius*: the category of 'missionary' is not an early medieval one, but rather a modern catch-all, in which religious figures of various kinds have been enshrined" (247). In a similar manner, Peter Brown refers to various missions and missionaries throughout *The Rise of Western Christendom* only to state toward the end of his massive work, "The idea of the 'missionary' seems so normal to us that we have to remember that it was only in this period [the eighth century] that anything like a concept of 'missions' developed in Western Europe" (414).

Yet, this kind of qualification is the exception. The overwhelming and unqualified impression presented by the majority of historians is that mission language belongs to an ancient time and culture, and it exists as part of a belief structure of ancient people. And yet, such a universal and general imposition of mission on events and people endangers the essential narrative of history.

Mission as History. Adolf Harnack (1851-1930) begins *The Mission and Expansion of Christianity in the First Three Centuries* with the lament that "missionary history has always been neglected" by historians of the church (xi). Yet quite possibly mission has been neglected as a form of history not because it is hidden, but because it is a modern phenomenon that arises at the height of the expansion of Protestant missionary efforts, and results from the need to account for the expansion of the Protestant church into new territories. Until the age of expansion, the history of Christianity was known as church or ecclesial history. With the differentiation of Christianity in Europe from the evangelizing efforts in the rest of the world, one history becomes two: church history and mission history. The *history of the church* is what happens in the historic places of the faith, such as Europe; the *history of mission* is what occurs at the margins, such as India and Japan. Church history and mission history, according to Andrew Walls, "do not just represent different periods, but different *kinds* of history" (1991:146). In other words, the function and nature of mission history is different from that of church history. Each serves a purpose, and one may, at times, contravene or contradict the other. What is evident is that mission history emerges as the need grows to explain, defend, and promote Western church expansion.

For mission to offer a credible explanation of Western Church expansion during the colonial era, it must find roots in Scripture and demonstrate its continuity from the earliest days of Christianity. Mission, used in this way, serves the needs of the Western church in framing a Western narrative of church within Christendom and legitimizing its expansion to territories beyond its borders.

When mission history consolidates the expansion of the church into a single history, simply known as Western, Catholic, Protestant, or Orthodox, it neglects other stories, other histories that were already in existence and expanding. Philip Jenkins reports that alongside the medieval church in Europe, there was “the much wealthier and more sophisticated Eastern world centered in Constantinople. But there was, in addition, a third Christian world, a vast and complex realm that stretched deep into Asia” (3). The rise and fall of these Christian worlds, each with their own political, religious, economic, social, and demographic hues and tones, is greater than mission and wider than mission history. Mission tends to refer to expansion in terms of Christendom assumptions (Europe as the only true center of the faith) and privileges the history of the European church over other histories. Mission becomes the simplification of a complex, varied story of Christian expansion into the rest of the world. To represent the expansion of Christianity as mission history is to ignore the rich diversity of traditions and stories, dynamics, and forces.

From its beginnings, Christian history has been not a single history but *histories*, tied to the traditions of the Western church, Catholic, Protestant, and Orthodox, which have chronicled the extension of their particular doctrines and practices throughout the world. While distinctions between these traditions is appreciated by those within, those on the receiving end view each particular extension as the whole of the Christian tradition. This is reinforced as each preaches and teaches their tradition as the true narrative of Christian history. Thus, mission history becomes the means of telling the story of a particular tradition’s expansion into new territories.

An increasing number of historians acknowledge the diversity of Christian expansion and insist that history is more than the extension of churches within a particular tradition. History, they insist, must account for a wider, more global history. According to

Kwame Bediako, "absolutisation of the pattern of Christianity's transmission should consequently be avoided and the nature of Christian history itself be re-examined" (116). And yet, mission history, all too often, creates the mistaken illusion that Christianity was established exclusively by outside agents and neglects the role of the cultural insider, often countering or even negating this wider, more diverse story. Mission history tends to perpetuate the notion that local expressions of faith were illegitimate or inept, and thus missionaries were necessary in order to correct or replace existing faith.

Andrew Walls characterizes the new task for the historian and students of Christian history as a re-visioning of the multitude of processes whereby Christianity became established (2002:3). Central to this task is the necessity of addressing the assumptions inherent in mission language. For example, mission promotes distinct spatial language of "centre" and "periphery" and thereby perpetuates a Christendom view of the world. Instead history should be written from the periphery and represent local issues and narratives rather than distant issues and narratives. For historians such as Walls, it is no longer appropriate to frame history as a movement from the Western center of Christianity to the "mission field." While Western mission is part of the story, it not *the* history of the churches in Africa. What Western Christians label as "mission history" sounds a great deal like "colonial history" in the ears of Africans, South Asians, and Latin Americans. Mission history as the expansion of the Western church anticipates that real churches that look and sound like churches in the West, will eventually appear all over the world. It is believed that successful mission will result in churches in India and Ethiopia adopting the history of churches in London and Dallas. Once they grow up as churches, they will be folded into the Western church narrative.

Because Christendom assumptions are hard to reverse, mission history remains in place. And yet, in the new age of World Christianity, the emerging global church is challenging the notion of mission history. As non-Western churches come to prominence and write their own histories, mission history becomes less and less important and may disappear altogether. “African and Asian and Latin American Church history,” Andrew Walls reminds us, “is not the same as missionary history; in itself, the missionary movement is a product of Western Church history” (2001:23). Mission history matters only as it offers prologue for local histories and critiques the exploits of the Western church. Dale Irvin suggests that rather than locating the history of Korean Christianity within the history of Western mission history, one must now “tell the longer narrative of Korean history, in its full religious and cultural formations” (133). I would add that this is well and good, as long as Koreans are writing this history, from a distinctive Korean perspective. As Christendom assumptions continue to collapse, mission as history will become more of a difficulty and less of a viable voice.

Mission as Grand Narrative. Narrative is the organization of events and actors in such a manner to convey chronology and development. The success of Christianity, according to Stephen Neill, is due to the fact that it “alone has succeeded in making itself a universal religion” (1986:4). The language of “universal religion” communicates a centered and uniform religious system that eventually triumphs, as it moves from a provincial faith to the faith of the empire and eventually to a universal religion. It is the spread of bishoprics and churches outward in an ever-increasing expansion. Latourette opens his seven-volume history with a similar narrative objective. "Geographically," Latourette asserts, Christianity "has spread more widely than any other religion in all the millenniums of mankind's long history." Because Christianity has penetrated every environment, "the story must include the spread of Christianity into all the people and regions where it has had adherents" (1.ix). Neill and Latourette's narratives are well and good, until their plot is given a name.

Mission provides Neill and Latourette with more than a narrative structure for history. Mission *is* narrative. Mission *is* plot. And thus, it is the scheme that forms events and characters into a narrative of universal triumph.

Yet the mission narrative is not the sole narrative at the historian's disposal. Historians from varied viewpoints have written capable histories of Christianity from vantage points other than mission. For example, Robert Bartlett in *The Making of Europe* argues that the plot for the expansion of the faith is Latin Christianity (250-55). The thrust of the faith is unity in and obedience to the Roman See, and thus papal authority. Eventually the line of identity drawn between Christian and pagan becomes the line between Latin Christianity and everyone else. To the Irish, Patrick was a Roman Christian – not a missionary. In the eyes of the pagan Friesians, Boniface was a representative of Rome-centric Christianity, not a missionary. Thus, expansion of the faith was in an essential way the encounter between heathendom (*paganismus*) and Christendom. What mission historians and missiologists have identified as missionaries are for Barlett diffusers of the Roman *brand* of Christianity over against other brands of Christianity or non-Christians ethnic identities.

In its assertion as the sole narrative of history, mission claims the role of grand narrative. And yet, the expansion of Christian faith is not one grand narrative of any type. From its beginning, expansion has been a confluence of multi-faceted narratives. These chronicle in unique ways the birth of the Christian faith in the Middle East and its rapid establishment in the surrounding cultures and languages. Such a confluence is even seen at Pentecost. We read of "Jews living in Jerusalem, devout men, from every nation under heaven." The Christian faith, from its beginning, was a diverse narrative. The vitality and rich history of the church in places beyond the Latin West, such as Persia, North Africa, Egypt, Ethiopia, and India, prior to 1000 AD, counters the claims that there was one governing plot from which the Christian faith expanded. Christian faith was poly-centric from its beginning, and the faith radiated not from one narrative and in one direction, but from many directions and many locales, languages, and expressions. According to Peter Brown, "Europe was only the westernmost variant of a far wider Christian world, whose center of gravity lay in the eastern Mediterranean and in the Middle East" (2). More than a mission from a central point, the faith was, in fact, a multi-directional movement.

Christianity as "universal religion" or a Roman-centric faith communicates that those who become Christian must find themselves compressed into or formed by this one narrative. And while mission communicates the universalization of Christianity as a religion, the Christian faith itself resists such compression, as it has translated itself into local languages, identities, and narratives.

Mission as grand narrative denigrates localized faith narratives and disregards the vibrant translatability of the Christian faith.

Rhetorical Confusion

The rhetoric of mission provides ample opportunity for historians and readers alike to generalize mission in such a way so as "to slip into romantic error" (Brown:30). Generalized language crowds a bewildering array of initiatives, activities, and actors into a single category. A telling example of this kind of generalizing absorption is Adrian Hasting's assessment of the period from 150 to 500 AD. Beginning with Patrick and ending with Boniface, Hasting's summation is that the "missionary centre of Western Church" is established in the western islands of Britain and Ireland (72). "Missionary" allows Hasting to offer an inexact, broad conclusion that asserts a particular (idealized) narrative about the progress of Western Christianity. Mission as generalized language fails to distinguish between a range of ideas and phenomena, does not offer qualification or specification, but compresses these into a convenient category.

Etic Language. Mission language also confuses, because it is seen from the outside or etic perspective. An emic orientation, on the other hand, offers an "insider" view from those who are participants in events or presents the perception of immediate eyewitnesses. Because the etic perspective is an outsider's look at events, persons, and entities, it can at best be a reinterpretation or restatement.

Mission is not the language of insiders, such as Patrick, Columba, Boniface, or Gregory, and thus it is etic. When an attempt is made to compress insider and outsider perspectives into one uncomplicated and uncritical history, the etic will trump the emic.

Inflated Language. Mission language confuses, because it says more than it should, inflating the intent of actors and the meaning for events beyond their original purpose. Mission language often highlights what should remain hidden and hides what should be brought to light. In many cases, persons classified as missionary are *pereginantes* (wanders). These are religious individuals outside the mainstream of the convent, monastery, or established ministries of the church who move to the margins for various reasons. To identify Patrick as a "distinguished missionary" and Dominicans as the "first 'missionary society' in history" repurposes who they were and what they contributed, all for the sake of the mission narrative.

Modern Rhetoric. Because mission and missionary do not come into use to describe the church's encounter with the world and its actors in this encounter until Ignatius and the Jesuits, both are modern, rhetorical innovations that provide proper and accurate interpretation of events and individuals but only when used for the modern era.

When the shift in rhetoric is not respected and a backward application of mission is made to Scripture, the early church, and medieval history, errors in judgment, interpretation, and application follow.

Partisans and Apologists will assert that there is little reason to disqualify mission just because it cannot be found in Scripture or the early history of the church. They maintain that many words essential to the church and in wide use today cannot be found in Scripture or the early church. And they are correct. The chief example, of course, is "Trinity." Invented by Tertullian, the actual word "Trinity" (*Trinitas*) is not found in Scripture but becomes the normative term to describe the pattern of divine activity and person found throughout Scripture. Similarly, "mission," they argue, is a distinctive term that emerged as an expression of biblical ideas and a signal of the action of God and the early church. They claim that if mission is disqualified as extra-biblical language, then Trinity as well must be disqualified.

Yet, while mission and Trinity might at first glance seem to be an appropriate comparison, they are not. The histories of the two words are quite different. Trinity enters Christian vocabulary quite early in Christian history out of the necessity to describe the complexities of "three persons, one substance," while mission, in its current use, emerges much later at the beginning of the modern era.

The retrospective reading of mission into Scripture and history as described in these first four chapters presents difficulties, but the decisive issue is not an anachronistic reading of mission into Scripture and history but the mentality, worldview, or framework this reading imposes. The assumptions present in Trinitarian language have been the subject of theological debate and councils throughout the centuries. And thus, the Trinity has been continually refined and reaffirmed but determined to be helpful, even necessary, for the church. My contention is that mission has been revised and reaffirmed without sufficient examination of its origins and assumptions. My intention in the following chapters is to move beyond the symptoms mission presents to a diagnosis of the source and cause of its problem.

A simple analogy illustrates the mission condition and what I hope to accomplish. If the water that comes from the tap in my house tastes and smells bad, I am going to assume that something is wrong with the water. I will either ask people in my city responsible for water safety to remedy the problem, or I will call a plumber to inspect the pipes in my house. If a city official or a plumber, without inspecting the source of the water or the pipes, simply told me to put an additive in the water or put a filter on the tap to improve the taste and eliminate the smell, I would be less than satisfied. While an additive and a filter may remedy the symptom, I would not be convinced the cause of the taste and smell had been adequately addressed. I would want a full and thorough investigation. Quite possibly, petrol or diesel has made its way into the water system. If the taste is metallic, then quite possibly lead from old pipes is contaminating the water. Or if there is a strong sulfurous smell, there could possibly be chemicals or human waste in the water. My ultimate concern is not how the water looks, smells, or taste. I want to ensure that my water is not compromised and the health of my family is not at risk. In the pages that follow, I am asking whether mission merely requires revision and rehabilitation (additives and filters), or if in fact the language is contaminated. While I have hinted at this greater problem several times in the discussion to this point, it is now time to trace the emergence of "mission" as both a conceptual framework and modern tradition, and to explore the difficulties in its origins and development as this modern term.

Part II

INNOVATING MISSION

5. Holy Conquest

Whoever therefore shall carry out this holy pilgrimage shall make a vow to God, and shall offer himself as a living sacrifice [...] and he shall display the sign of the cross of the Lord on his front or on his chest. When, truly, he wishes to return from there having fulfilled his vow, let him place the cross between his shoulders; in fact, by this twofold action they will fulfill that precept of the Lord which he prescribed himself through the Gospel.

Eyewitness report of Pope Urban II's words at Clermont, November 1095

The general opinion is that those living in Catholic Europe during the Middle Ages responded to those outside Christendom in one of two ways. On one side is Christendom's violent assault on Muslims and Jews, known as the *crusades*, and on the other is the expansion of the Christian religion by way of preaching and charity, known as *mission*. Often these two, crusade and mission, are characterized as polar opposites, each with a different aim, and yet existing alongside each other. However, the language of the age reveals a multitude of approaches with a variety of means and a wide range of terms. Chief among these is the language of "pilgrim" and "pilgrimage." While pilgrim language traditionally described those who moved voluntarily beyond the bounds of Christendom, it was coopted by the church to mobilize Catholic Europe to march on Jerusalem. In this shift, pilgrimage evolves from an inward and peaceful disposition of movement and alienation to one that is outward and militant. The aim of this new kind of pilgrimage is the capture of Jerusalem and the establishment of enclaves of Latin Christianity in the Levant. Pilgrimage becomes the language of utility to propel Catholic Europe toward the world beyond Europe, and it is the soil from which mission eventually emerges.

Urban's Summons

In November 1095, Pope Urban II (1042-1099) assembled the council of bishops at the city of Clermont in the French Auvergne, where he preached one of the better-known sermons in history in which he called on bishops and laypeople throughout Catholic Europe to march on the Holy Land. Eyewitnesses report that his principal message was a summons to liberate Jerusalem from the control of Muslims and the rescue of Christians in the East. Urban's grand cause was to take up the cross, battle against the Saracens, and conquer Jerusalem. According to reports, those present responded with shouts of *Deus lo volt* – God will it or God wants this. Would-be crusaders then cut pieces from their garments in the shape of a cross and attached these to their shoulders signifying that they accepted the cause to liberate Jerusalem and were thus following the injunction of Jesus Christ to take up their cross and follow him. With his sermon begins what has come to be known as the First Crusade, calling Catholic Europe to a holy war against an enemy 2000 miles away.

A number of forces and factors prompted Urban's call for a crusade. The most obvious and immediate was a plea from Byzantine Emperor, Alexius 1 Comnenus (1057-1118), to the Pope and his subjects to aid in Constantinople's defense against advancing Turks. The second was the idea of liberating the holy places of the East that had been desecrated or destroyed by "the enemies of Christ." Both aims were couched in the language of holy pilgrimage, words that resonated with and gave cause for rulers, knights, clergy, and ordinary people from across France, Germany, Italy, and England to set out for the Holy Land.

The thought of a pilgrimage to liberate Jerusalem so enthused the populace of Catholic Europe that many set out before the official start of the expedition (August 15, 1096). Bands of pilgrims spontaneously gathered with spouses, children, and belongings and made their way toward Constantinople. Estimates of those who answered Urban's summons range from 50,000 to 136,000, depending on whether the number represents only fighting men or also includes non-combatants (Riley-Smith, 1987:11; Tyerman:147).

Within four years of Urban's sermon at Clermont, Turkish forces holding Jerusalem were defeated, a Patriarch was installed in the Holy City conducting the Mass in Latin, and European settlements were established in the Levant. During the two centuries that follow, more armies assembled and march across Europe to the East, fighting against the enemies of Christ. The rhetoric of mission and missionary was not used to describe this encounter. Instead, pilgrim language resounded in Urban's sermon and was the cause to which Catholic Europe responded.

The practice of pilgrimage to the Holy Sepulchre in Jerusalem, as the supreme act of penance for sins, was familiar language for what became the crusades. In fact, the term crusade was unknown at the time of Urban's sermon. Not until the thirteenth century were wars to conquer Jerusalem described as *crozeia*, *crozea*, or *crozada*, after the most prominent symbol of its fighters, the cross (Tyerman:29). The English word "crusade" was supplied only in the eighteenth century. Instead, this new venture was described with many different words of motion or movement, such as *iter* (journey), *via* (way), and *via Dei* (way of God). But above all, the movement to rescue the church of the East and retake the Holy City was spoken of in terms of a *peregrinatio* (pilgrimage) and those who responded were designated as *peregrini* (pilgrims). The exact words of Pope Urban's sermon have not survived, but those present report that his call for a holy war was encased in the ancient language of pilgrimage.

The basic meaning of Latin *peregrinus*, dating back to the time of Cicero, carries the idea of being foreign or alien. Thus, those who go on a pilgrimage are strangers who take up a journey to a foreign place. Pilgrims of the religious sort are not mere wanderers or travelers, but they make pilgrimage with the purpose and intent to gain merit through acts of privation and prayers and to worship at sacred sites.

Pilgrimage activity is central to the Judeo-Christian tradition. The Hebrew Scriptures recount Abram setting out from his homeland and family to a new land. The Israelites sojourn in the Sinai on their way to the Promised Land and, in their Babylonian exile, they long for their return to Jerusalem. These Jewish roots are background for the Christian tradition of journeying into foreign lands and to sacred places. Luke writes of pilgrimage at the outset of the Christian church, as devout Jewish men and women from various nations travel to Jerusalem for the Feast of Pentecost. Peter describes the existence of early Christians as aliens and strangers or sojourners, as does the writer of Hebrews speaking of those who exhibit faith as "strangers and exiles on the earth [...] seeking a country of their own. [...] they desire a better country, that is, a heavenly one" (Heb 11:14, 16). "Pilgrim" and "pilgrimage" describe many of those who ventured forth and preached the gospel in new and strange places, some by choice others because of persecution. In pilgrim and pilgrimage, we find ancient language of movement, intersection, exile, and cause.

Augustine, in *The City of God*, distinguishes Christians as those who live as "pilgrims journeying toward the Lord," and as such they make "use of earthly and temporal things like a pilgrim in a foreign land" (19.17). Pilgrim language gives identity that, in some ways, supersedes language, race, and ethnicity, and gives the person a new name, identity, and cause.

Unique contributions to the Christian understanding of pilgrimage come via the Irish. Distinctive cultural understandings of pilgrimage among the pre-Christian Irish entered existing pilgrim practices for Catholic Europe, making pilgrimage more than a journey to a shrine or holy site, or a defining identity, but "a process of alienation" (Webb:7). The pilgrim cuts himself off from the familiar, home, and family, and establishes himself as an alien in a foreign community. This kind of denial of self and relocation to a foreign place ostensibly turned into witness and the extension of the Christian faith.

With Urban's summons, the ancient tradition of pilgrimage became aggression, and while the meaning changed, the language of pilgrim and pilgrimage remained.

Before the crusades the way of devotion and imitation of Christ had been a withdrawal from the world, a monastic calling, to go into a desert to live as ascetics, to retreat to a cave to seek God, or to be cloistered in an island community. Now laymen were given something to do that was almost equivalent to applying the monastic ideals of crucifying self and taming mortal desires. The "unsettled populace" was able to take the cross as a means of imitating Christ. Donning the cross and journeying to Jerusalem became, for the warring pilgrim, ways of conquering the world, the flesh, and the devil. They lived a pilgrim existence as they abandoned wives, children, and work, fasted before major campaigns, made displays of public piety and devotion, and risked their lives through privation, exposure, and battle. Once in the Holy Land, they visited holy sites and venerated relics, all as acts of piety and in fulfillment of their vow. In these ways, the populace was able to mimic traditional pilgrim vows.

While knights and foot soldiers were part of the march to the East on the First Crusade, the bulk of those who responded were unorganized, undisciplined common folks wishing to become pilgrims. Pilgrimage became both a privilege and an obligation for the whole of Catholic Europe, rather than the choice of a few.

Traditionally, the pilgrim would take a vow to make a pilgrimage, and upon fulfilling the vow, his or her sins would be absolved. The crusader vow was in effect the pilgrim vow. Each was a spiritual exercise, with a spiritual outcome. The vow was not fulfilled until the pilgrim fought for the liberation of Jerusalem and then worshiped at the Holy Sepulchre, or died trying.

Traditional pilgrimages were undertaken as part of the commitment of the devoted. In many cases, a pilgrimage was initiated because the person had been instructed to do so in a vision or because of a crisis in their life or a feeling of guilt. Urban's sermon marked a change in the manner in which pilgrimages were initiated, no longer from compulsion but from persuasion, whose goal now was to become one marked with the cross or a cross-bearer (*crucesignati*). The cross became powerful mobilizing imagery. No longer was the person simply part of the general Catholic populace, but he or she was a *crucesignatus* who wore the cause of Christ in a bodily form. Taking the cross turned a private matter into a public event and made it binding.

For many, taking the cross meant death. Whereas indulgence "was a gift from God, martyrdom is the martyr's gift of his own life. It was so great an act of merit that it justified the martyr immediately in God's sight. Baldric reports the words of Urban's Clermont sermon: "And may you deem it a beautiful thing to die for Christ in that city in which He died for us."

Urban's summons to pilgrimage was more than a call to prayer and fasting but to violent acts against the enemies of the cross. With Urban's summons to an armed pilgrimage, the giving of one's life became the taking of another's life. Much like accounts in the Old Testament, crusading pilgrims saw themselves as God's army tasked with the assignment of taking the Holy Land from God's enemies.

The paradox that Jesus taught peace and love for one's enemies and the cross as symbolic of his self-sacrifice, rather than the slaughter of others, did not seem contradictory, and the violent liberation of Jerusalem was admissible because Urban, Christ's representative on earth, sanctioned holy pilgrimage as assault.

Early critics of traditional pilgrimages, such as Augustine of Hippo and Gregory of Nyssa, pronounced them to be dangerous because the journey to the physical Jerusalem became the chief point, and the journey to the heavenly Jerusalem was diminished or lost. For them, a focus on the earthly Jerusalem was a distraction from the eternal Jerusalem. And yet, from the beginning of the church, pilgrimages to Jerusalem were regularly made by small groups and occasionally by the lone ascetic. Increasing in the eighth century through the influence of the Celtic Church, and the Irish by the tenth century, conditions had improved for travel through Italy, allowing for larger and more frequent groups of pilgrims to set out for the Holy City. Another reason for the increased interest in pilgrimages was the millennium celebration of Christ's death and resurrection (1033) that drew a flood of pilgrims to Bethlehem and Jerusalem.

Catholic Christians believed that because Jerusalem had been the place of Christianity's beginning, it would be the place of its culmination (*parousia*). It was from Jerusalem that Christ sent his disciples to make disciples of all nations, and naturally this mandate would find its fulfillment in the same physical spot. The crusading pilgrim was contributing to and participating in the return of Christ. Pilgrimage became a means of establishing the kingdom of God on earth.

Pilgrimage language was more than indicative of these changes. Pilgrimage converted violence and aggression into virtue and piety. Unsavory ends were justified by holy means. Pilgrim language recedes in succeeding crusade accounts, and yet the changes to the concept of pilgrimage itself remained and provided context and cause for mission language that was to come.

6. Latin Occupation

The crusades were not missionary ventures but wars of conquest and primitive experiments in colonization.

Paul Johnson, A History of Christianity

Holy pilgrimage resulted in Latin colonies. Chief among the consequences of Urban's summons was the establishment of enclaves of Latin Christianity in Syria and Palestine, where many of these later pilgrims stayed. Once Jerusalem, Antioch, and other cities were captured, the planting and sustaining of Latin colonies became the goal, and the stage was set for competing visions of church and state to clash.

Pope Urban's policy was to work in concert with Emperor Alexius I Comnenus and respect the historical place of the eastern churches. Yet rather than an expansion of a united Christendom, captured territories became Latin ecclesial and political domains. Local Christians and their longstanding rites and traditions were replaced and pilgrimage became the Latinization of eastern Christendom. As Catholic Europe extended its presence in the centuries ahead, the church continually sought ways to re-exert its influence and control.

Christendom, decreed earlier by Charlemagne as a territorial identity, was solidified as a corporate identity through Urban's holy pilgrimage. Christians worshipping in other languages and via other rites and those of other doctrinal positions were brought into Western Christendom as they submitted to the Latin Rite, and its enforcement was the sign of the West's domination and control. Entrance into European identity came via the ecclesial language of Latin.

For Christians in the East, the establishment of Latin political administration and an ecclesial hierarchy was the beginning of 200 years of Latin domination. Any hope of healing the split of 1054 was dashed by the unilateral actions of the Catholic conquerors and was completely destroyed in subsequent crusades. Different expressions of Christianity came into direct conflict. In a letter written to Urban following the defeat of Turkish forces at Antioch, crusade leaders confessed, "we have overcome the Turks and heathens; heretics, however, Greeks and Armenians, Syrians, and Jacobites, we have not been able to overcome" (Fulcher of Chartres:68).

The linguistic and communal identity for Catholic Europe became a territorial description known as Christendom, as opposed to a surrounding "heathendom" and to regard the expansion or extension of Christendom as a praiseworthy goal. As rulers conquered in the name of the church, new subjects were incorporated into the Latin Church. Latin became the signature of this identity and the bridge over which new peoples, apart from Muslims, found their way into Christendom. Christendom was Latin Christianity. Greek Christianity was not Latin Christianity, and thus, it too came under attack and was brought under Latin control for a period.

For Muslims, who were not in direct contact with the margins of Catholic Europe but located at a distance, the crusades served to solidify rather than weaken their identity. The physical and social margins were great and thus the chance of being converted and acculturated into Catholic Europe was highly unlikely. The strength of position and firm religious conviction gave Muslims the resolve to resist and eventually repel the invading forces.

The rare attempts to convert Muslims were usually mixed with coercion and penalty. And yet love was not absent. In papal encyclicals and sermons of apologists for the crusades, words such as *caritas*, *charitei*, or charity are prevalent, but "the idea of the crusader expressing love through his participation in acts of armed force was an element in the thinking of senior churchmen in the central Middle Ages" (Riley-Smith, 1980:177, 188). Ultimately, violence was characterized as an act of Christian charity.

Augustine provides the rationale for violence as love (19.12). His conviction was that force was necessary, and even commanded by God, in order to express true love to those who were heretics. Just as a parent disciplines a child, or a physician must take severe measures in order to heal a person's malady, so force must be applied by the Christian upon those in error and even to the enemy. While uneven and inconsistent in the period leading up to the First Crusade, the sentiment of the crusader toward the Muslim was that they convert or die.

Mission and Crusade

The language of "mission" is simply non-existent before and during the crusades. Because persons called "missionaries" do not exist and thus cannot be sent, missionaries are not active among Muslims. Mission, as organized and concerted efforts of evangelization in the modern sense of the word, is not named by those inside or outside the church to describe the activities of Christians toward non-Christians. Whatever the motive, they are crusaders and not "missionaries" sent by mission entities, nor were they sent under the banner of "mission."

Modern interpreters of the medieval era and the crusades find reason to liberally insert "mission" and "missionary" into the narrative of the crusades. However, in this appropriation, they ascribe nineteenth-century assumptions and aims to eleventh-century events and individuals. Some interpreters imply continuity between mission and crusade, and others explicitly state it, and thus the Muslim world associates Western imperialism and Christian missionary work with the Crusades.

Two figures that stand out more than any others during the crusading era, into whose lives mission language has been inserted by subsequent interpreters, are Francis of Assisi and Ramon Llull.

Francis of Assisi (c. 1181-1226) is often cited as the chief example of a medieval missionary who opposed the crusades. The basis for these claims is his encounter with the Sultan of Egypt. During the battle for the port of Damietta (1219) in the Fifth Crusade (1217-1221), Francis approaches and tries to convert the ruler of Egypt. This incident is offered as a clear example of mission and a missionary approach as distinct from crusading. Stephen Neill writes of Francis' "missionary zeal," the "missionary methods" he instituted, and the "missionary enterprise" that resulted in the founding of the Franciscan order (1986:99).

Yet none of the early chroniclers describe Francis' encounter as "mission" nor do they name Francis a "missionary." Francis is identified as a Christian, messenger, cleric, holy man, "intrepid knight of Christ," "man of God," "the friend of Christ," shepherd, servant, and pilgrim, but not a missionary. When one looks to St. Francis' writings, mission language is absent, and it is not found in early Franciscan sources (Finnegan:3). Francis' journey to Damietta is described as a "pilgrimage." Because he is delayed on the way to Jerusalem, and thus waiting at the crusader encampment, he decides to cross the battle lines. His encounter with the Sultan is unanticipated and unplanned. Thus, his action is not against crusading. Rather, he seeks to proclaim the gospel and wants to become a martyr.

Ramon Llull (c. 1232-1316) of Majorca has been described as the first and still the greatest missionary to the Muslims, and Stephen Neill notes that Llull was "the first to develop a theory of missions," and ranks him as one of "the greatest missionaries in the history of the church" (1986:114-15). Yet he describes himself as pilgrim, friar, hermit, man of God, and servant of God, but not a missionary. To inject mission language into Llull's story is improper and even subverts an accurate assessment of his intentions with his publications, and his witness to Muslims.

The seeds of mission may have been germinating in the soil of Medieval Christianity with such figures as Francis and Ramon Llull, but it is with the birth of another order, the Society of Jesus, that mission emerges as a modern rhetoric.

7. Mission Vow

> *Since one's being sent on a mission of His Holiness will be treated first, as being most important, it should be observed that the vow which the Society made to obey him as the supreme vicar of Christ without any excuse, meant that the members were to go to any place whatsoever where he judges it expedient to send them for the greater glory of God and the good of souls, whether among the faithful or the infidels.*
>
> *Ignatius of Loyola,* The Constitutions of the Society of Jesus

Mission, in its modern meaning and use, made its appearance in the sixteenth century when Ignatius de Loyola (1491-1556) took existing language and repurposed it for a modern use. He took mission – *misión* in Spanish and *missio* in Latin – and extended its meaning and intent. But Ignatius did more than coopt an existing term and give it new meaning, mission offered Ignatius a medium through which his ideals and commitments meshed with the notions and spirit of his age. From Ignatius' introduction of mission into the speech of the Society of Jesus, a major shift began that eventually reformed the way in which the church talked about and framed its encounter with the world. In Ignatius' innovation, the era of mission began and the modern mission movement has its roots.

The Montmatre Vow

On the Feast of the Assumption, 1534, Ignatius and six young men gathered to celebrate mass in the monastery chapel at Montmartre on the northern side of Paris. Ignatius was the center of gravity around which the others rallied, including Francis Xavier (1506-1552). They had linked themselves with Ignatius by way of his guidance through his unique devotional practice called the *Spiritual Exercises*. As each took Holy Communion, they made solemn vows to poverty, chastity, and the intent to journey to Jerusalem, placing themselves at the disposal of the pope to be sent wherever he assigned them.

Four years after their gathering at Montmartre, Pope Paul III (1468-1549) established the Society of Jesus. Their vows of poverty and chastity were not unique, but the *votum de missionibus* or the mission vow, known specifically as The Fourth Vow, defined the new order and gave it the dynamism necessary to become one of the most powerful forces for the expansion of the Roman Catholic Church. Their vow to the sovereign pontiff declared that they would "go anywhere His Holiness will order, whether among the faithful or the infidels, without pleading an excuse and without requesting any expenses for the journey, for the sake of matters pertaining to the worship of God and the welfare of the Christian religion" (Loyola, 1970:79-80). The Montmatre vow to be pilgrims became the mission vow that formed the Society into a frontline force for the Latin Church.

Before Ignatius, the words of choice for the expansion of the faith had been "evangelizatio," "propagatio Christianae Fidei," and "Fides propaganda" (Clossey:13). The common element in each of these was the spread of the faith – i.e. to evangelize non-Catholics and to propagate its Catholic form, but no one term or phrase dominated. Abruptly, mission, as a way of describing the movement of people to assignments, in order to proclaim the Christian faith, made its debut. Interpreters of the Jesuits describe Ignatius' introduction of mission language as "a shift," "an innovation," "a crucial discursive breakthrough," and a "daring conception" (Kollman:426, 427, 429; O'Malley:4; Guibert:149). Ignatius' turn to mission language was more than an adjustment or tinkering with a side issue. Ignatius describes mission as "an end eminently characteristic of our Institute," and "our starting point and principal foundation" (1970:267).

Missio, Misión, Missão, Mission

Ignatius did not create "mission" but instead appropriated an existing word and filled it with fresh intent and meaning. As he does not offer an explanation for this refashioning of established language, we can only infer why he adopts mission. In Ignatius' context, mission was in use in four languages and with multiple meanings: *missio* (Latin), *misión* (Spanish), *missão* (Portuguese), and *mission* (Old French). These uses were active parts of Ignatius' world of language and thus easily employed.

First, Latin *mitto* and *missio* were terms in use to explain the inner workings of the Trinity. While Trinitarian expressions of Father, Son, and Spirit were part of the language of the early church from the beginning, Irenaeus, Tertullian, and Augustine developed fuller theological statements of Trinity. *Mitto*, as a common verb, designated the action of the Father who sends the Son. As in the New Testament and early church writing, the common sense meaning of *mitto* is to throw, send, or dispatch. Augustine also uses the noun form to reference the mission of the Son of God (*missio filii Dei*) as does Thomas Aquinas (1225-1274), who does not extend its use to the church or human agency but restricts his use of the term to the Trinity. It would have been natural for Ignatius to appropriate a term previously restricted for the sending of Christ in order to identify his and the actions of the Society with those of the Triune God.

Second, *misión* and *missão* were terms to describe the diplomatic and military activities of Iberians in foreign lands. Agents of the emperor acted as personal envoys, reporting only to him and representing his wishes. As this administrative system developed, these envoys or representatives were further classified as *missi minores* and *missi majores* (Thompson:17).

Third, the Old French word *mission* (*mession*, *mecion*, *mision*, *mesion*) was in wide use and was the etymological source for the Spanish word *misión*. In Old French, mission meant "expense," "cost," or "outlay," conveying a sense of obligation, and thus it was a legal term of obligation between parties for a monetary agreement.

Though Ignatius does not indicate his source of "mission" or why he makes it the defining tenet of the Society, what is obvious is that forms of "mission" were in wide use and thus easily adopted without explanation. Ignatius exploits the various uses of mission, but he also expands their meanings.

Ignatius' World

Ignatius' vow of mission and Pope Paul III's approval of the Society are part of the Latin Church's response to the changing political and ecclesial landscape of the late medieval period where the notions of *conquista* (conquest) and *padroado* (patronage between the Pope and Spain and Portugal) were important elements that shaped Ignatius' mission language.

Conquista. In 1498 four ships from Portugal with red crosses aglow on white sailcloth arrived off the Indian coast. With their arrival, Vasco da Gama (1469-1524) opened the eastern sea-route to India and thus moved Portugal into a position to dominate the lucrative trade of spices and silks. While the Portuguese were not the first Europeans to venture eastward, da Gama's appearance there initiated a new period in history, marking the beginning of Western dominance throughout Asia. The Portuguese, along with the Spanish, led the way, with the Dutch, French, Germans, and British to follow, and as they touched the far corners of the globe, they established a political, military, mercantile, and ecclesial presence.

Running throughout these motives was an anti-Muslim sentiment, an extension of the crusade spirit of the previous era as European powers sought ways to check the Muslim political and economic advance. The eventual establishment of Portugal's political and commercial rule in India meant the expansion of control over both Muslim and Hindu subjects.

Economic, political, and strategic motives did not exist solely unto themselves but were imbued with religious aims. The Roman Church played its part in expansion by providing sanction for the state's political and commercial aims and in turn the Church was able to advance its cause. What was generally acknowledged was that "religion supplied the pretext and gold the motive" for European expansion (Cipolla:101).

The Latin Church sought the power of the state because of threats on two fronts. First, the long-standing threat of Muslim powers had to be addressed, and second, the new reality of a fractured and warring Christendom brought about by the Reformation required a realignment of power. Spanish and Portuguese ships and trade were the right antidote for both Muslim and Protestant threats.

The Portuguese saw expansion as a patriotic crusade, with Portugal as the standard-bearer of the Faith. These campaigns were more than Portugal's self-assertion but a defense of the Latin Church and central to the church's expansion.

In Stephen Neill's assessment, European expansion of the sixteenth century belongs under the headings of "Crusades, Curiosity, Commerce, Conversion, Conquest and Colonisation, in that order" (1984:87). Where the Iberian empires traveled, the Latin Church followed. The church's intent to Christianize followed in the footsteps of the crown's aim to Latinize. The two paralleled and served each other, and for those who received Vasco da Gama, Latin Christianity arrived in his ships.

Padroado. The crusading spirit remained a defining force for the church well into the sixteenth century, especially in its collaboration with the Spanish and Portuguese crowns. A series of papal bulls reinforced a crusading spirit of a united Catholic Europe and reflected the church's power to call princes and emperors to common causes, and sanctioned the subjugation of newly discovered native peoples to the Latin Church.

"The right of conquest" was the exclusive permit for Portugal to explore, colonize, exploit, and Christianize wherever they might land. The mandate of the *padroado* to bring the lands discovered and their peoples into the Christian faith gave ecclesial sanction to, and justification for, the civilizing mission undertaken by Portugal.

The reach and power of the crown's *misión/missão* beckoned the Latin Church to reach beyond Europe as well, and its response came in the form of Ignatius' mission vow. Mission became utility for the church, and the Jesuits served as its ground force as the church expanded. Portugal and Spain, *conquista* and *padroado*, and existing language are the context in which Ignatius innovates "mission." These provide the impulse for what emerges as the Ignatian mission.

8. Ignatian Mission

I promise special obedience to the Supreme Pontiff in regard to the missions as contained in the bull.

Ignatius of Loyola, 1541

The founding papal bull and constitutive documents of the Society of Jesus are a reflection of the changing context and adjustments in the church-state relationship. *Misión* and *missio* appear in the Society's founding documents, and thus "mission" becomes unique language for the Society's way of proceeding in the world. And yet, mission is more than the church's adjustment to the changing situation. It emerges from Ignatius' personality and life experience.

Ignatius' adoption of mission language is motivated by ideals of chivalry, mystical visions, and his desire to make pilgrimage. As a young man of Navarre, Ignatius was not a career soldier, but a courtier trained in the art of diplomacy and the use of weapons. His desire to soldier became a reality when in 1517 the viceroy of Navarre, Antonio Manrique de Lara, called Loyola into military service. "For almost four years Ignatius filled his days with jousts, the chase, business of the duke, and the continued reading of romances," until the Navarrese finally marched for Charles V against the French at Pamplona (Bangert:4). The battle turned against the Navarrese, and their position seemed to be lost. While most of the soldiers thought it folly to defend the fortress of the city and felt it necessary to surrender, Ignatius stood firm. He rallied those present to make a stand. But their defense of the citadel was short-lived as Ignatius was struck with a cannon shot that shattered his right leg. Ignatius' days as a soldier ended almost as quickly as they began.

Following the surrender, Ignatius was taken back to Loyola where his leg underwent surgery in order to correct the terrible job done on the field at Pamplona. Pain and severity of the situation initiated his turn toward faith and his life of service. While convalescing from his second surgery, Loyola requested books about "knight-errantry," but as there were no books on chivalry and "knightly romance" at hand, he was forced to read books about the saints and their devotion. These books included *Vita Christi* (*The Life of Christ*) which presents Christ as a medieval king who conquers and reigns.

Ignatius' desire to imitate the life of the saints grew until he came to the conclusion that as soon as he recovered he would go to Jerusalem. His change of heart was complete following a night vision of Mary, standing before him with the holy child Jesus. This turned his worship and service toward Mary and Christ.

His journey to Jerusalem was one in which he gradually stripped away, piece by piece, his former life. He exchanged his fine clothes for those of a pilgrim, made his confession, and left his sword and dagger at the altar of a pilgrim church. He did not completely abandon the ideals of chivalry and glory, but transferred these to the spiritual realm as now a soldier of Christ at the service of the Holy

Mother on pilgrimage to Jerusalem. Here he began composing the *Spiritual Exercises* which mirrors the rigors of preparation for military service and became the means by which one is to discipline oneself as a new soldier of Christ. During this time, a group of like-minded men became his companions. As a society, they vowed to place themselves at the service of the pope to go wherever he wished, in absolute obedience and personal allegiance.

In 1537, while on his way to Rome to present himself to the pope, Ignatius and two colleagues entered a small chapel. During prayers he sees Jesus carrying the cross and the Father at his side. This vision recorded by Loyola in *Spiritual Journal* not only connects his activity with that of Jesus but also couches this connection in terms of mission. The connection of his actions and those of the Trinity gives Loyola's commission and, more specifically, ties his mission to the Trinitarian life of God. The message for Ignatius in this vision is that he is to live in service with the Trinity. It is with this confidence and upon this mandate that Ignatius and his companion arrive in Rome and establish the Society of Jesus.

Whereas the "apostolic way" up to Loyola's day had been one of Christian contemplation and perfection within one's self, Loyola conceives of it as movement toward others in service and suffering. The aim had been to imitate the apostles, and thus there was a powerful "nostalgia" for the early Church, sharing a communal life with all things in common and renunciation of the world. The chief desire was to return to a purer, more perfect life that entailed a renunciation of the world, contemplation, and self-mortification in communal life. With Ignatius, contemplation and devotion were still present and active parts of his form of the apostolic life, but for him spirituality was a means to an activist end. Jerónimo Nadel, assistant to Ignatius, characterizes this sentiment: "We are not monks [...] The world is our house" (O'Malley:68). The Jesuits were not the first nor were they alone in this modification of the apostolic life, combining action with contemplation, service with penance, but the identification of these actions as "mission" is unique to the Society of Jesus.

While the physical journey to Jerusalem was the chief way in which Ignatius had conceived pilgrimage, it was not to be restricted to this dimension alone. Pilgrimage could mean to visit a shrine, to go into exile, and to preach. What begins as pilgrimage to the Holy Sepulchre expands to the whole of his life, to serve the needs of people wherever they found them. The set of guidelines for those who had become Jesuits was known as the *Regulae peregrinatium*, or "Rules of Pilgrimage." Pilgrimage, for Ignatius, was mission.

Ignatian Mission

The beginnings of the modern use of mission lies within Ignatius' innovation, but "mission" as conceived by Ignatius must remain in the sixteenth century and rest within Ignatius' personality and initiatives. Because mission included any place to which the pope might send members of the order, this most often meant being sent to locations within Europe, and only occasionally to places beyond its borders.

The first members sent on a mission went to nearby Siena to reform a monastery in that city. In these cases, mission meant preaching, caring for those in hospitals, hearing confessions, and serving the poor. Xavier was the first Jesuit to venture beyond the bounds of Europe under the new designation of mission. King John III of Portugal requested of Pope Paul III via Don Pedro Mazcarenhas, his ambassador in Rome, for priests from the Society of Jesus to be deployed to India. The Pope deferred by stating that such a risky undertaking could not be commanded but only undertaken voluntarily. So, the ambassador took the request directly to Ignatius and, in the end, Ignatius agreed to send two of the Society, Simón Rodrigues and Francisco Xavier. Ignatius told Xavier, "The work is yours." To which Xavier replied, "Pues, sus! Heme aqui!" (Good [Splendid], I am your man!)

Xavier went to Goa and for a decade labored along the coast of India, Ceylon, Malacca, Japan, and on the fringes of China. In December 1552, he died on the island of Sancian off the mainland of China.

With Xavier and these meager undertakings, the mission era began. In a matter of years, Jesuits extended their presence beyond India, Japan, and Macao to reach around the world. The initial company of ten grew to a thousand by Ignatius' death in 1556 and over 20,000 by 1700. What Ignatius initiated grew into a worldwide organization and marks the beginning of mission.

The letters of Francis Xavier, written before his departure for India and immediately after his arrival, do not mention "mission," and it is only years after his arrival in India that Xavier refers to those the Society sends out for the work of carrying the gospel to the heathen as "missionaries" and their work being that of "mission." It is in the evangelization of the Americas, chiefly by Franciscans in the seventeenth century, that other terms become less prominent and "mission" becomes the word of choice, and in due course, triumphs over all other words and becomes the preferred way of describing the expansion of the faith. In the Jesuits' introduction and use of mission, a monumental shift occurred in the language and meaning of the church's reach beyond Christendom. Ignatius' innovation and Xavier's voyage initiated the modern mission era.

Part III

REVISING MISSION

9. Protestant Reception

My brothers and sisters, today is the day of missions.

Count Nicolaus Ludwig von Zinzendorf

At the time Ignatius innovated mission, a schism was taking place in Western Christianity. Among the differences between the Reformers and the Catholic Church was "mission." For Protestants, mission had to shift from a designation tied exclusively to monastic orders and Roman Catholicism to a term signifying a movement that included all types of people. In this eventual shift, mission expanded in meaning to include more than Ignatius intended and the Catholic Church could imagine. And yet, concepts and images inherent in the original innovation of mission endured and made the long journey from Ignatius to the Protestant tradition.

Many modern Protestants assume that the Reformers spoke and wrote about "mission" from the beginning. While the Catholic Church may have been late in coming to mission language, surely the Reformers were quick to adopt "mission" and eager to declare their commitment to the cause. And yet, such assumptions would be wrong not just in terms of the Reformers' practice but also in their conceptual framework.

Critics of the Reformers' hesitancy toward mission are quite severe. Gustav Warneck and others assert that Protestantism of the Reformation era lacked any missionary activity or sentiment, adding that the Reformers showed no concern for overseas missions to non-Christians. It is very difficult to find one real missionary venture on the Protestant side during the sixteenth century, and mission was absent in the Reformers' words, actions, and "*world of thought*" (Warneck:6). Latourette measures the Protestant mission activity in light of robust Roman Catholic mission endeavors and finds Protestants lacking. Among the reasons for their delay, he mentions the Reformers' all-consuming task of redefining the faith and reforming the church (2.25-27). Doctrinal issues, ecclesial roles, and ritual practices were their first order of business. Furthermore, they were preoccupied with internal conflicts, had no monastic system in place, lacked contact with non-Christian peoples, and their sponsoring governments were indifferent to the spread of the Protestant faith. And yet, in defense of the Reformers, Bosch argues that it is unfair to expect them to subscribe "to a definition of mission which did not exist in their own time" (249).

The level of the Reformers' proselytizing activity might be open to debate, but what is certain is that mission language was absent among Protestants during the early years of the Reformation. "Mission" and "missionary" were not adopted until the early eighteenth century and did not become established until the nineteenth century. One looks in vain throughout the works of Luther, Calvin, and other early Protestants for the language of mission or missionaries.

Martin Luther (1483-1546) raises the question of the gospel going into all the world, but he does not prescribe particular actions or designated roles regarding the evangelization of those outside Europe. Should a Christian find himself in a place where there are no Christians, "he needs no other call than to be a Christian, called and anointed by God from within. Here it is his duty to preach and to teach the gospel to erring heathen or non-Christians, because of the duty of brotherly love, even though no man calls him to do so" (310). He does write of sending in such terms as *sendung*, *senden*, and *missio*. In the case of *missio*, Luther identifies the provenance of such sending as *Dei*, *Patre*, and *Spiritus*, not human activity in general or the church in particular (Huhtinen and Lockwood:16-17). The most that can be said is that Luther emphasizes the reform of the church and the spreading of the gospel, and thereby provides the foundation for the eventual reach of Protestants beyond Europe. Luther's concern is not the justification or promotion of mission. Luther states that the gospel is universal and thus includes Jews, Turks, and those classified as heathen, but he does not label the universal nature of the gospel as "mission" or those who preach to Jews and Turks as "missionaries."

Though John Calvin (1509-64) does not write specifically of mission as a definite action of the church and missionary as a role for Christians, he does make reference to the mission of Christ, the mission of reconciliation, and the mission of the twelve apostles. The world beyond Geneva is a concern for Calvin, and involvement in that world is evident in his writings, but this concern and call for the church's involvement is not expressed in mission language. Yet, Calvin is often cited in attempts to establish an early Protestant mission legacy. He did cooperate in the selection of ministers who were sent to Brazil to found a Christian colony, but the request was for pastors for oversight and care of the Huguenot settlers rather than for missionaries.

Thus the writings of Luther and Calvin contain rich theological language that generates Protestant witness and service beyond Germany and Geneva, but mission rhetoric is foreign to their vocabulary, although in these Reformers we find theological foundations for the eventual launch of the expansion of the Protestant faith, but this comes a century later.

Adrianus Saravia (1532-1613), lauded often as an early champion of the Great Commission, makes this appeal in language other than mission, and nowhere in his 1590 treatise are "mission" and "missionary" found. Others label Justus Heurnius (1587-1651) as an early Dutch pioneer in mission thought and identify him as a missionary. After petitioning the East India Company and the Dutch Church to send him overseas, Heurnius was sent to Jakarta, Indonesia, in 1624. The claim for his role as a mission pioneer is largely made on the basis of the title of his 1618 book, *An Exhortation, Worthy of Consideration, to Embark upon an Evangelical Mission among the Indians*. Though mission appears in the title of the English translation, *missio* or *missiones* is not in the Latin, and neither does he use "mission" in the book to describe the work of Christians or the church. And yet, Heurnius' book is characterized as "missionary writing," and Latourette indicates that through Heurnius' appeal "a missionary seminary was established at Leyden which in the succeeding ten years trained twelve youths who were sent as missionaries to the East" (3.43). So while he is an early and important sign of the rising tide of mission as a concept for Protestants, he is not an early adopter of mission rhetoric.

Justinian von Welz (1621-66), an Austrian nobleman, wrote a number of tracts in which he opposed dominant opinions within Lutheran orthodoxy and proposed the sending of witnesses by means of a society. His treatises are interpreted as "missionary documents," and he is characterized as "an early prophet of mission;" but for Welz, mission is what Roman Catholics do in the "propagation of their false teaching," and thus he associates the word with Catholic activities (Welz:62).

Savaria, Heurnius, and Welz push the boundaries of Protestant involvement in the world beyond Europe by taking reformation theology to its conclusion. And yet, these harbingers of the "mission concept" do not employ mission language or simply mimic Catholic mission structures. It is important to draw these fine distinctions in order to demonstrate the Catholic roots of mission and identify the points at which Protestants differed. These distinctions are in part what causes Protestants to delay in adopting mission language.

Interpreters consider Anabaptists to be the singular group among the sixteenth century reformers with the most developed missionary impulse and theology. Yet, while the Anabaptists may be noted for their distinct concept of mission, mission language was not part of their confessions or early writings. Rather, they viewed themselves as pilgrims and martyrs. Early Anabaptists did not use mission partly because mission carried with it territorial implications and, unlike Catholics, church for them was contrary to notions of land and sacrament. Furthermore their evangelizing activities were more spontaneous and informal than organized, and when they eventually sent their members in a systematic manner, they designated them not as missionaries but "apostles."

Stephen Neill notes that for Protestants "there was little time for thought of missions," as their attention was on the reform of the church located in Europe rather than in places where the church was not (1986:187). And unlike the Catholics they did not have the organizational framework or resources at hand to initiate mission structure or activity.

The Protestant hesitation to use mission language stems firstly from the fact that it was a Catholic innovation tied to the Roman church and Catholic political powers. In many places, this arrangement meant Protestants were the recipients of Catholic mission effort, some of which included forced re-conversion. Protestants had to make their own start with mission, but theirs would be from another starting point and via a different route.

Protestants also hesitated to use mission on theological grounds for they saw mission as an endeavor that interfered with God's activity. The use of temporal means to accomplish eternal divine work was theologically untenable to Lutherans and Calvinists. At the heart of the Protestants' hesitation to adopt the language of mission was their understanding of church. Witness took place in their home location and, therefore, mission as a foreign endeavor was irrelevant. Not until Protestant countries began their own expansion of commerce and rule did the church of the Reformers adopt language necessary to describe the church's geographic expansion. Then again at a time when a massive and thorough reform of the church was underway the Reformers did not wish to burden their understanding of church with extra-ecclesial language, and "mission" for Protestants was a non-ecclesial term.

The Rhetorical Turn

In spite of these barriers, mission gradually made its way into Protestant language and eventually became part of its vocabulary. The most serious indictment against Protestantism's lack of mission practice and language came from Robert Bellarmine (1542-1621), a Cardinal and Jesuit theologian. He dismissed Protestants as not being the true church, for while thousands of Jews and Turks have converted to the Catholic faith, "the Lutherans have scarcely converted one (to the Protestant faith), although they compare themselves with the apostles and evangelists, and they have many Jews in Germany, and in Poland and in Hungary there are many Turks nearby" (13).

Another force that pushed Protestants toward mission language was the colonial aspirations of Protestants. Their adoption of mission rhetoric coincides with the quest of Protestant countries for colonies, and the ensuing need for organizational methods for the church to accompany them. Just as the colonizing effort of Spain and Portugal facilitated the expansion of the European Catholic Church, initiatives by Dutch and British commercial and political entities, such as the East India Company, did the same for Protestants. Soon after Protestant countries expanded their political and commercial reach, mission language appears in the titles, charters, and sermons of societies. Rather than arising solely from theological conviction, mission emerges with Protestant colonial aspirations and the need to organize and religious interests abroad.

The occasion for the entrance of mission language into the Protestant vocabulary was the rise of voluntary societies. Modeled after independent commercial enterprises already operating in colonies, societies expedited the entrance of Protestants into these same areas. Societies did what Protestant churches were ill-fitted and incapable of doing, and thus societies provided a convenient way for mission to become Protestant language without becoming ecclesial language. The Protestant view of church as an autonomous, local body, loosely affiliated around doctrinal convictions, meant its churches were provincial and locally focused. When convictions about the universal nature of the gospel emerged and forces from outside pressed for overseas involvement, these churches did not have structures, means, or outlook to make a response. So while Protestants did not create the language of mission, they innovated the mission society as their unique response to the world.

Protestant societies did not start out explicitly as "mission" societies. Early societies used the language of propagation, foreign and heathen, in their charters and titles. The earliest of these, the Society for the Propagation of the Gospel in New England (1649) and the Church of England's Society for the Propagation of the Gospel in Foreign Parts (1701), opted for words other than mission and missionary. The charters of these early Protestant societies listed a wide range of activities, such as "to promote Christian Knowledge," but mission as a description of the society's work was absent. The stated aim of these societies was the care for white settlers from England rather than preaching for the conversion of the native population. They sent chaplains rather than missionaries. In many cases, the evangelization of local inhabitants was only incidental and even prohibited.

When the Society for the Propagation of the Gospel in New England was established in 1649, one of its initial undertakings was to raise funds for the work of John Eliot (1604-1690). Celebrated today as one of the first Protestant missionaries and named as the "Apostle of the Indians," Eliot migrated from England to the Massachusetts Bay Colony in 1632. While pastoring a church, he became concerned for Indians in the surrounding area, learning their language and evangelizing a number of them. He established Christian Indian towns, and translated the Catechism and the Old and New Testaments into the Algonquin language. The new society viewed Eliot as a way to fulfill its charter, and thus brought him under their sponsorship. Though in every way representative of modern mission activity, the charter of the society and Eliot's work were not described as "mission."

The Society for Promoting Christian Knowledge (SPCK), founded in 1698 by John Bray (1656-1730), began for the purpose of printing and distributing educational materials for schools in British colonies. Bray modified the society's name and charter in 1701 to reflect widening interests. In its new form, King William the Third granted corporation to The Society for the Propagation of the Gospel in Foreign Parts with the charge to minister to "loving subjects" in British colonies and to combat "Romish Priest and Jesuits [who] are the more encouraged to pervert and draw over our said loving subjects to Popish superstition and idolatry" (Humphreys:xxvi). The Society's original charter does not use the word mission, nor does it refer to those who carry out the duties of the society as missionaries but as "officers, ministers and servants." Yet, in a pamphlet of the society published in 1700, *A Memorial Representing the Present State of Religion, on the Continent of North America*, mission language is evident and frequent. Bray argues for "a sufficient numbers of proper missionaries" to counteract the efforts of "Papists" among the colonists. Following his survey of each of the colonies, he concludes that 40 Protestant missionaries are needed. An early history of the Society published in 1730 by David Humphreys, Secretary of the Society, names throughout his accounts the agents of the Society as missionaries, but refers in general to "the Work" or "the Trust" of the Society (16, 18, 20). He uses mission sparingly as a means to describe the activities of traveling preachers, as well as the overall work of the Society. With Bray and the SPCK, "mission" is introduced into societal language but not as a central statement of the society's purpose.

The growing concern among Protestants for non-Christians in foreign lands and the desire to send people to preach the Christian faith solidified, and became explicit mission language with the Danish-Halle Mission and the Moravians. The Royal Danish-Halle Mission, founded in 1704, later known as the Tranquebar Mission, was the first society with mission in its title and thus signals the institutionalization of Protestant mission rhetoric. In all likelihood, this initiative originates from the Danish crown, rather than from urgings of the Danish Lutheran Church which maintained that the gospel was sufficiently preached by the apostles throughout the world and believed the Danish Church had no right to place uninvited ministers, except in areas where the Danish King ruled. The royal charter placed the Mission under sponsorship of the Danish crown, and thus, it's support came from the Danish government and not the church. Because the Danish crown administrated the affairs of the Danish citizens in the colony, as well as the Indians in Tanquebar, the Mission operated under the principle of *cujus region ejus religio*, the religion of the ruler is the religion of the ruler's subjects. Thus, the first explicit Protestant mission society followed a pattern already established in Portuguese and Spanish Catholic efforts.

A collection of letters from the first Danish missionaries, Ziegenbalg and Plütschau, provides an account of their journey to India and the difficulties they encountered. Mission language is used throughout. This introduction of mission language has a ripple effect throughout Protestantism, chiefly through the publication of its missionary reports. The first to follow suit were the Moravians.

The Moravians, or Herrenhuter, went throughout the world with the aim "to win souls for the Lamb." The combination of their exilic outlook and Pietism, mediated to them by way of Augustus Francke (1663-1727) and Nicolaus Ludwig von Zinzendorf (1700-1760), produced an unusual outlook on the world and a zeal for Christ. As a result, Moravians sent Brethren from Herrnhut as early as 1732 to work among African slaves in the West Indies and with Eskimos in Greenland. The first Moravians did not go as religious professionals or "missionaries" but as a potter and carpenter. By 1740, 86 of their community had been sent, and at the time of Zinzendorf's death twenty years later, over 300 had left Herrnhut for places such as Greenland, Georgia, Labrador, West Indies, and Africa. The number of those sent from Herrnhut and the places where they landed had an astonishing effect on the whole of Protestantism. Their exploits influenced both John Wesley and William Carey, and inspired Protestants throughout Europe.

From the beginning, Zinzendorf's theological outlook included "all humanity," yet, initially he does not frame this as mission. He describes early Moravians sent from Herrnhut as witnesses, servants, and disciples, and they did not depart Herrnhut with the designation of "missionary." Instead, they went via their trade and craft, and thus they were known as weavers, brewers, and carpenters. It was only after the initial period of sending that Zinzendorf switched to the language of mission.

Mission and missionary do not appear in the first two volumes of Zinzendorf's *Hauptschriften*, but both enter his writings and addresses by volume three. A 1746 discourse entitled *Vom Grund-Plane Unserer Heiden-Missionen* opens with the declaration, "My brothers and sisters, today is the day of missions" (3.186). For Zinzendorf, the main difference had been that sending from the congregation of Moravians and the endeavors of the Danish-Halle Mission were not the same. Whereas the Danish Mission was founded for the specific purpose of mission, the Community of the Brethren existed to "help individuals love the Savior and meditate on his merits" (Atwood:62-63). Just as Ignatius innovates mission language for the Roman Catholic orders, Zinzendorf and the Moravians introduce mission as ecclesial language for the Protestant Church. Nevertheless, Zinzendorf does not equate mission with the church or the community. He implies that there is a significant difference between state-initiated and state-sponsored mission through a voluntary society and the Community of Brethren.

Eighty-seven years after the founding of the Danish-Halle Mission and sixty years after the sending of the first Moravians, British Baptists constituted The Particular Baptist Society for the Propagation of the Gospel amongst the Heathen (1792). The name of the society was shortened almost immediately to the Baptist Missionary Society. Following the Baptists, other societies soon followed: the London Missionary Society (1795), the Edinburgh and Glasgow Missionary Societies (1796), the Anglican Society for Missions to Africa and the East, later known as the Church Missionary Society (1799), and the Wesleyan Missionary Society (1813).

In its fundamental nature, Protestant mission emulates Catholic mission and through these extra-ecclesial entities, *corpus Societatis*, mission makes its way into the mainstream of Protestant speech. Thus in the course of two centuries, mission moves from questionable language to an established tradition and the Danish-Halle Mission, Zinzendorf, and the Moravians play catalyzing roles in enabling this transition.

10. Missionary Problems

The end of the conference is the beginning of the Conquest.
The end of the planning is the beginning of the Doing.

John R. Mott, Edinburgh Missionary Conference of 1910

The earliest recorded use of mission in the English language referring to persons sent by religious groups or churches to proselytize others is by Francis Bacon in *An Advertisement Touching on Holy War* (1629). In this pamphlet, Bacon poses a fictitious debate between five persons concerning whether it is lawful for Christendom to engage in holy war for the expansion of Christianity. In Bacon's use, mission operates alongside the state in the expansion of the church. Just as the state has its forces for expansion, the church has its sword. Over the course of two plus centuries, Bacon's singular notion of church expansion takes shape in societies and grows in dimensions and usages, until it develops into a tradition – the modern mission movement. From a single word expressing the action of the church, a tradition denoting a modern movement arises.

The modern mission movement – definite article, two adjectives, and a noun – represents a set of historical occurrences imbued with religious, social, national, and emotional connotations. Movement, the noun, denotes a common ideology, belief, or system. An array of religious, political, and social movements, either from the past or in the present, provides examples of what movements might look like and what they do. Some of these movements have been social (Women's Suffrage Movement), religious (the Jesus Movement), or still others are political (the Civil Rights Movement). Just as adjectives qualify other movements (the Environmental Movement, or the Suffragist Movement), "modern" and "mission" likewise qualify this particular nineteenth-century movement with particular meaning and tone and give it definition. The first adjective, *modern*, places the movement in a particular period of history, beginning at some point in the sixteenth century, and characterizes it as shaped by Enlightenment ideals. *Mission*, on the other hand, gives the movement a purpose that can be general and undetermined, but in this case, points to the expansion of the Christian religion. The definite article identifies movement as known and distinguishable, and thus, particular and historical.

The modern mission movement functions like any other identity, motto, or slogan, as "an instrument of continuity and of change, of tradition and of revolution," and thus, it is a reminder of the recent past and a call for a response (McKeon:2). In this way, the modern mission movement structures reality, and maintains and advances specific perceptions and values for individuals and the church. While significance can be found in each of the three words (modern, mission, movement), taken together they offer a distinct concept that frames identity and cause.

At some point early in the nineteenth century, "the modern mission movement" came into use. The first appearance of the phrase in print coincides with the centenary celebration of the founding of the Baptist Missionary Society. Louis A. Banks in an article published in 1889 for *Zion's Herald* describes the modern mission movement as "a century plant," and locates its origins in the "agitation" of William Carey (330). The following year, Oswald Dykes, in an article entitled "The Modern Mission Movement," celebrates the force and labor of the movement begun with Carey and notes that the idea is still progressing with "sobriety" and "improved position" (38). Two years later, 1892, the phrase appears once again in reference to the mission efforts of the Baptists. In all three instances, the phrase refers to a movement one hundred years old, initiated with the founding of the Baptist Mission Society, and marked by the departure of William Carey from England for the distant shores of India.

British Baptist historian, Ernest A. Payne, characterizes the history of British Baptist mission effort as "the story of the modern missionary movement." While Payne admits that there were forerunners to the movement in the persons of Frances Xavier, John Eliot, David Brainerd, Moravians, and John Wesley, these were only foreshadows of what was to come in the Baptist Mission Society. He makes clear that it is with Carey and the formation of the Baptist Society for Propagating the Gospel among the Heathens that the modern mission movement begins. Leon McBeth identifies Carey's booklet, *An Enquiry into the Obligations of Christians to use means for the Conversion of the Heathen* (1792) as "the charter of the modern missionary movement" (185). While Baptist historians locate the inauguration of the modern mission movement narrowly with British Baptists, non-Baptists make the same assessment.

Not only are Baptists placed at the head of the modern mission movement, but William Carey is named as its father. Yet some claim that lesser-known, non-English speaking individuals rather than Carey should be placed at the head of the modern mission movement. Among these, Catholics assert that St. Francis and the founding of the Mendicant Orders are the beginning of the modern mission movement.

However none of these early pioneers, including William Carey, claimed this distinction for themselves or used the phrase. At some point in the later part of the nineteenth century, ideas and activities coalesced into the notion of a movement that was both missionary and modern, and thus, the modern mission movement came to designate the way in which modern Christians described the encounter with the world beyond Europe and America. The phrase has stretched into present day use in such a manner that it has become a modern Protestant tradition.

A Modern Tradition

While the modern mission movement refers to historical events, it is less than a historical occurrence or an actual movement. It functions somewhat like a belief, connecting people and organizations to a defining ideology that forms the basis for collective belief and action. Key ideas and devices contribute to the invention of the modern mission tradition.

First and foremost, the modern mission tradition finds justification in ideas from Scripture. More than just the notion of mission as the Great Commission, the apparatus, techniques, institutions, and organizations of the modern mission movement are justified by reference to biblical figures and Scripture passages and themes.

Second, among the symbols of the modern mission movement are exemplary persons. Such heroic individuals as William Carey, Henry Martyn, Hudson Taylor, and Lottie Moon embody the values and spirit of the movement. The founding acts of the movement can be found in the imagery of young William Carey at his cobbler's bench with leather maps of the world on the walls and the meeting of ministers at Kettering where Carey pleaded with Baptists. These lives and their actions have grown to mythological proportions, providing a powerful narrative for many of the beliefs of the tradition.

Third, the invented tradition is built on a line of progenitors, represented in individuals and groups, that can be traced back through the Medieval period and Constantine to Paul and the early church. Nineteenth-century mission literature chronicles their lives and substantiates the portrayal of "missionary" as an established tradition.

Fourth, mission magazines and journals, mission biographies, and popular mission histories are public monuments to the movement's founders and heroes. The study of these publications by women and children groups, in churches and societies, as well as families at home, reinforces themes and ideas and advances the narrative of the movement. In addition, these impart the tradition to potential supporters and practitioners.

Fifth, funding mission through pledges and offerings provides opportunity for wide voluntary participation and thus a low threshold for "joining" the movement. No matter how small the amount or infrequent the contribution, participation in the cause can occur for anyone. One of the functions of the growing number of societies in the modern era was a forum for wide participation in the modern mission movement via small, incremental giving, which reinforced the educational process of instilling the tenets and history of the tradition.

Sixth, mission conferences are platforms to recite the progress and triumphs of the modern mission movement and thus reinforce the tradition's narrative where tales of exploits and victories are recounted. Toward the end of the nineteenth century, a host of student or general mission conferences were held with increasing regularity.

Seventh, the modern mission tradition establishes an alternative narrative highlighting the expansion of the Protestantism in the modern era over that of Catholics and the Orthodox Church, and one whose legacy stretches back to the New Testament era.

Finally, slogans encapsulate the spirit of the mission tradition in compact, pithy statements which continually reinforce the ideals of the mission tradition. The watchwords of the Student Volunteer Movement, "The Evangelization of the World in this Generation," and of the World Missionary Conference, Edinburgh, "World Evangelization in our Generation," communicate that the fulfillment of the tradition was possible and even imminent.

By the opening of the twentieth century, the modern mission movement was firmly fixed as a Protestant tradition and represented the new orthodoxy. In reading the Scripture through the "missional lens," the modern mission movement was made sacred and established its legacy in the early church and the Bible. Through a variety of means the modern mission movement became a tradition.

The Missionary Problem

A number of early mission conferences were large and broad in scope, but they were only a prelude to the grand gathering of 1200 delegates in 1910 at Edinburgh. The gathering was predominately male and Euro-American with only a handful of representatives from Asia, Africa, and Latin America, with no delegates from the Catholic and Greek Churches or the Catholic missionary orders. Mission was the central concern of participants from across the world and hundreds of correspondents whose contributions formed the reports of the Conference's eight commissions.

The Edinburgh Conference is often noted as a turning point in Christian history for a number of reasons, but above all it is the high point of the modern mission movement and a benchmark for mission rhetoric in the twentieth century. The Archbishop of Canterbury, Randall Davidson (1848-1930), emphasized the necessity of a response in the presence of such an unparalleled event in human history. In Davidson's words "The place of missions in the life of the Church must be the central place, and none other. That is what matters" (*WMC*: 9.142). John R. Mott (1865-1955), the chief organizer and chair of the Conference, proclaimed to the delegates that mission was a modern enterprise whose time had come.

Speaker after speaker justified and historicized mission as more than just right or proper but as a mandated obligation. Presenters declared Paul, Barnabas, and Jesus, as missionaries along with Augustine Boniface and St. Francis. Mission was theologized: "God is the great Missioner," and thus mission is a divine enterprise (*WMC*: 1.351). Edinburgh was the high point for mission rhetoric and established the pattern for how Partisans in the years following would mobilize personnel and resources for the mission endeavor. Mission language filled the Conference hall. It was the idea whose time had come, the emblem of right belief, and the language of the faithful – a sacred Christian tradition.

Reports, addresses, and discussions at Edinburgh and before refer continually to the missionary problem: *The Missionary Problem* (1883), *The Missionary Problem – Home and Foreign – and its Solution* (1896), *Students and the Missionary Problem* (1900), *The Key to the Missionary Problem* (1901), and *Islam in India as Modern Mission Problem* (1917).

Not that "mission" and "missionary" were problems. The missionary represented the progress and advancement of Christendom. Rather, the practitioners of non-Christian religions and natives were the problem because of their backward and pagan ways. Mission was steadfastly justified, but lukewarm churches and unrepentant Western representatives of corporations and governments were cited as among the impediments that hindered mission.

In the spirit of the Enlightenment, all problems were solvable through the missionary enterprise. And yet, in distinction to the Enlightenment, the solution did not lie in science, education, and technology alone, but must be accompanied by missionary utilizing these modern means.

The missionary problem needed to be solved by missionary work described in language that was militaristic in tone and words. The Archbishop of Canterbury opened the Conference with language reminiscent of the Jesuits. He addressed the delegates as "Fellow-workers in the Church Militant, the Society of Christ on earth"

(*WMC*: 9.146). John R. Mott summarized this sentiment clearly in the Conference's final address. He closed with the pronouncement, "the end of the conference is the beginning of the Conquest. The end of the planning is the beginning of the Doing" (*WMC*: 9:347). In the rhetoric of Edinburgh, vestiges of Urban's summons to march on the Holy Land and Ignatius' militia for Christ that conquered for the glory of God could be heard. The legacies of aggression and conquest inherent in mission were evident in the language of Edinburgh.

Mission as conquest continues following the Conference, as Mott and others promoted the vision and hope of Edinburgh. Sherwood Eddy, a participant at Edinburgh, offered a retrospective look 35 years after the Conference from "the far-flung battle line of missions" and characterized the task as "nothing less than a missionary crusade." He acknowledged that the crusades of the eleventh and twelfth centuries were "sordid affairs of slaughter and lust," "a strange mixture of good and evil," but persisted in his depiction of missionaries throughout the ages and pioneers of the mission movement as crusaders and in his call to the present world missionary crusade (5-7, 11). Mission for Edinburgh meant the world situation and its problems required the marshaling of the army of God for the conquest of the world.

Missionary Occupation. Those at Edinburgh viewed the world as divided into two spheres, Christendom and heathendom. The task of the "missionary societies of Christendom" was to "turn heathendom into Christendom" (*WMC*: 1.297, 424). The expressed aim was the occupation of more and more of the unoccupied fields.

The language of occupation and Christianization is akin to the Latinization of the Levant following the First Crusade and the subjugation of peoples in Spanish and Portuguese colonizing efforts. The establishment of outposts of Christian presence meant the arrival of Christendom in the midst of heathendom. One of the threats to missionary progress identified at Edinburgh was rising nationalism among colonialized people. It was feared that national identity and the revival of ancient religious traditions would harm the advance of Christian mission. Mission at Edinburgh meant the occupation and civilization of non-Christian lands and unchristian peoples.

Missionary Triumph. Hope for world evangelization and boundless optimism were the overwhelming sentiments of Edinburgh. Confidence ran high for the "triumphant power of the gospel" and the time for its "greatest progress" (*WMC*: 1.10).

The church's role was to provide the resources for mission, education for mission, and a context conducive for mission. Mission meant societies and boards, as these entities sent and supported missionaries. Mission entered the Protestant vocabulary as an endeavor outside the church and at the opening of the twentieth century remained at the margins of the church, in many ways dependent on the church and yet separated from it. Mission at Edinburgh meant the triumph of Christianity through societies – not the church.

The Problem of Mission

Within two decades of the Edinburgh Mission Conference, the problems *for* mission became the problem *of* mission. While the Edinburgh focus had been on the removal of all barriers that hindered the mission task, a host of factors, including a World War and worldwide financial collapse, soured Edinburgh's optimism and called mission into question. Uncertainties regarding mission emerged at the Jerusalem meeting of the International Missionary Council in 1928 and persisted into the next decade. With the financial backing of John D. Rockefeller and the initiation of a group of prominent laymen, a commission representing seven American denominations formed in 1930 to make "a new and thorough study of the basis and purport of missions and of their operations" (*Re-Thinking*:ix). The aim of the commission was no longer to address the problems facing the mission situation but to rethink "mission" itself.

The Report of the Inquiry cites declining funds and growing indifference as reasons for the need to reappraise mission. Yet, within the pages of the Report, other reasons are obvious. The Report criticizes various aspects of mission, such as types of tasks undertaken, the manner in which these are done, and the competency of personnel and the quality of their work. Rather than promoting mission activity and announcing the imminent triumph of the mission enterprise, the commission reviewed mission's presuppositions and probed the "widest possible consideration of the meaning of the mission enterprise" (*Re-Thinking*:x). What delegates at Edinburgh assumed, the commissioners of the Laymen's Inquiry questioned. The problem was no longer the obstacles that stood in the path of the mission enterprise, but whether these mission efforts ought any longer to go on. The chief question pursued by the commissioners was not about best methods, or a better use of resources, or the eventual triumph of the Christian religion, but the foundation and meaning of mission (*Re-Thinking*:x, 3).

In their appraisal of mission, the commissioners looked beyond piety and good works to the motives and quality of the missionary, and found many missionaries "of the finest spirit" with "traits of greatness and originality," but others they classified "as misfits, unable to cooperate, running more or less individual ventures, more often than not a discredit to the name of Christianity" (*Re-Thinking*:13). Yet, these critiques were peripheral, for something more than an evaluation of the efficacy of particular missionaries was at the heart of the Report. Rather than missionaries changing world problems, the totality of mission was evaluated in light of changes in the world situation.

Of the "sweeping changes" across the globe, the Commissioners focused on three: "an altered theological outlook, the emergence of a basic world-culture, and the rise of nationalism in the East" (*Re-Thinking*:18-23). Mission, the Report asserts, must account for the ongoing theological adjustments due to progress in scientific truth and philosophical concepts. Mission must accept that many of their services, such as education and health care, were no longer needed, and that mission was no longer the sole provider of these services. Mission must recognize that Western culture and institutions were viewed as defective in light of the Great War and rising nationalism. Common to these changes was the need to uncouple the Christian religion from its alliance with the power and prestige of Western culture. The Report indicated that such an uncoupling would occur when missionaries noted Christianity's claims of superiority and its language of conquest and occupation as deficient or misguided.

From their appraisal, the commissioners endorsed mission but they qualified their affirmation with the suggestion that there must be a change in the meaning of mission. The new emphasis would still be on communication of the high spiritual values of Christianity but in consideration of world unity, mutual understanding, and a shared civilization rather than merely conversion to the Christian religion. Second, it proposed that mission should move from a permanent occupation to one that is temporary. The rationale for the call to mission should issue from "the spiritual unity of men and races, the coming of the life of God into the lives of men, and the maturity and full measure of development of individuals and social groups," and not the perpetuation of organizations and their presence in countries (*Laymen's*:2.xxii). In these changes to the basic understanding of mission, Edinburgh's ideals of conquest, occupation, and triumph were on trial and judged as problematic.

In contrast to Edinburgh, the commissioners of the Layman's Inquiry are Revisionists, retaining the language of mission but creating alternative narratives. Soon after the publication of *Re-Thinking Missions*, Latourette claimed that if Christian mission is to survive, it "must be adjusted to the conditions of the day which is dawning." And yet, he proposes a revision of mission that is different from that of the Laymen's Inquiry. He declares, "Retrenchment must cease." Rather, there must be "thorough reconsideration and, where necessary, drastic revision" (1936:xi, xii, 125-27,155). Latourette was only the first of what has become a long line of Revisionists. From the 1930s until today, Revisionists have sought to retell the mission story as their narrative, and recreate the missionary in another image. Because of Revisionists, mission now can mean almost anything, and the meaning of mission is diffused and muddled.

The Inquiry made little difference to those who continued in the partisan affirmation of an Edinburgh version of mission. However, for those in ecumenical circles and involved in discussions associated with the International Missionary Council and the World Council of Churches, the question of mission persisted. As the title of the Report states, the Inquiry comes "After One Hundred Years," and appraises the condition of the modern mission movement from its beginning at the end of the eighteenth century to the early twentieth century. Whereas Edinburgh attempted to draw lines of continuity between current mission endeavors with activities of the Jesus, Paul, the early and medieval churches, the Inquiry only assessed the modern era. The Report hardly mentions New Testament or medieval mission endeavors. This omission suggests that the Laymen's Inquiry viewed mission as only a modern undertaking, and thus they called into question its biblical and historical validity.

In the wake of the Report, Apologists mounted arguments for continuity between the modern mission enterprise and the biblical and historical narratives. Partisans-turned-Apologists shifted from promotion and mobilization to justifying and historicizing mission. Before 1932, there had not been much need for such arguments, and thus works on the Bible and mission were sparse or rather thin in content. One of the few exceptions was W. O. Carver's *Missions in the Plan of the Ages* (1909). His objective in these printed lectures to students at Southern Baptist Theological Seminary was to counter the effects of higher biblical criticism and "speculative theology" which he viewed as discounting the Bible as the "textbook of missions" (20). After the publication of *Re-Thinking Missions*, books and pamphlets detailing the biblical basis of mission appeared from every direction. Cleland McAfee of the Board of Foreign Missions, Presbyterian Church, USA, attempted to answer questions emerging from the meeting of the International Missionary Council at Jerusalem in 1928 and to anticipate the questions raised by the

Layman's Inquiry in his book, *The Uncut Nerve of Missions: An Inquiry and An Answer* (1932). For McAfee, the crisis in mission was not with mission itself but with the lack of support and enthusiasm in home church, and thus, he sounded much like the delegates at Edinburgh.

However, the tone of other books and pamphlets in years following the Report was quite different. For example, Julian Love's concern in *The Missionary Message of the Bible* (1941) was with "stemming the tide of retreat," and criticized the Layman's Report as a source of this ebbing support. While attacks on mission had always existed, he saw the Report as "a much deeper and more trenchant criticism, cutting at the theology behind missions and at the basic purposes of the churches, and resulting in a confusion of the whole idea and program in the minds of leaders as well as followers." In the years following the Report, the theology of *Re-Thinking Mission* was most often cited as the chief concern in partisan responses, but rather than a theological counter offense, the tactic most often was to construct a bridge from the Bible to the modern mission enterprise.

As a modern tradition, seen as the remedy for the world's problems, the mission tradition itself became the problem. Because of the place of mission in Protestant rhetoric, the commissioners and the Report could not be ignored or dismissed but demanded response.

The Shift Underway

Partisans, Apologists, and Revisionists have honed their response to the crisis in mission. Partisans promote mission with vigor, and Apologists seek to defend mission via a host of means. Revisionists work to rehabilitate mission per current religious and cultural shifts.

The result is that mission is widely contested, and the word has created a confusing conceptual terrain. The shared problem for all three approaches is the persistent use of mission language itself. Rather than preserving or rescuing or revising mission as sacred language or a biblical concept, and attempting to reformulate the legacy of mission to suit modern sensibilities, it is time for a shift away from mission language. Such a shift is necessary because the heart of the "missionary problem" is the problem of mission language. It is time to recover ancient language that enables a more vibrant, more appropriate encounter between the church and world.

Waning Christendom signals that mission language should be abandoned. As Christendom recedes, Christianity as a centerless religion becomes more and more apparent. Europe is no longer the home or geographical bastion of the faith. America is not a Christian nation. Christendom, both as a territorial entity and ideological frame of reference, has passed into oblivion. The death of Christendom dispels the notion of sending to another realm, confronting and overcoming geographical barriers, and crossing the boundaries of Christendom into heathendom inherent in mission language.

The colonial legacy of mission is difficult to overcome and cannot be casually dismissed. Mission language is firmly rooted in the spirit of conquest and colonialization. An attempt to reframe, redesign, or reform mission does not erase these memories, nor does it rescue mission from its legacy. While mission may hold warm and positive historic meaning for some Christians in the West, the remembrance for many in the rest of the world is anything but virtuous or noble. Rather than helpful language that facilitates, mission is a liability that debilitates. Rather than creating possibilities and opening doors, mission limits and restricts. Rather than elucidating Scripture and the Christian tradition, mission misconstrues and distorts.

Pluralism ends the rationale for mission language. The missionary as an ecclesial agent sent from the place where Christianity *is* to another place where Christianity *is not* is no longer intelligible. In common vernacular, "mission" is usually foreign or international mission, and it includes travels or a trip. And yet, "over there" is no longer over there. Neighborhoods in the West are a highly diverse mixture of ethnicities, languages, and religions. One does not have to travel (or be sent) from Birmingham to India to meet a Hindu or to Japan to talk to a Buddhist. Hindus and Buddhists, as well as Muslims, Sikhs, and Animists, shop in local stores, go to school, and live alongside Western men and women and are, in fact, Western men and women themselves. Social and religious homogeneity are still possibilities but only as choices reserved for those with the means to live in gated communities and suburban enclaves. Modern European and American cities, such as London, Hamburg, Chicago, and Houston, are patchworks of different peoples created by migration, war, employment, and displacement. Pluralism is the new reality that makes mission language redundant.

As modernity declines so will mission. Introduced at the outset of the modern era, mission grew alongside modernity and embodied its ideas and sensibilities. Mission and modernity grew up together as siblings in the same household and thus learned from each other and mimicked the language and ways of the other. Each has family resemblance and traits of the other, because they share the same Enlightenment birthright. Mission is inhibiting its own progress with memories and ideas that have their origin not simply in the Bible, but, more specifically, in Western dreams of control and knowledge.

The concept of mission presupposes that Christian faith must move from a center where it is firmly established to those on the periphery where it is not. The fact is that Christian faith is now everywhere and even strongest in places where it was once the periphery.

Mission language perpetuates the belief that one form of Christianity is meant to dominate all others. Some counter that the Christianities that exist at the margins are not real or are less than orthodox Christian faith, and thus, the need for the right kind of Christianity. In other words, mission is needed in order to replicate a denominational brand or a narrow notion of Christianity. When used in this way, mission is another word for church extension, the spread of our version of orthodoxy or proselytization.

Today mission appears outside the West most often in places where there is a long and deep Western mission history. For example, mission language is quite prominent in Korea and India, because they have been schooled in its history. In contrast to this persistent use, mission language is under scrutiny in far more places throughout the world as a vestige of the colonial era, looking, feeling, and sounding like a worn project of the nineteenth and early twentieth centuries and loosing currency.

The search for authentic faith creates space for language other than mission. Rather than being laden with a foreign political agenda or replicating a Western pattern of Christianity, the exigencies of the present-moment demand that we live in solidarity with believers around the world. The legacy of mission is the uni-directional exporting and franchising of particular forms of Christian faith, rather than the mutuality of people being transformed by people who are themselves being transformed. Instead of merely delivering the Christian religion, the sentiment must be one of reciprocity in which we come to listen and learn from each other, be transformed by others. Solidarity and mutuality, either with those who live nearby or those faraway, enriches and enlivens transformative exchange. The shift is away from mission as one-way deliverables to an authentic faith exchange that transforms in both directions.

Future Shift

At the outset of the twenty-first century, both mission and the modern mission movement seem to be antiquated language retroactively applied to the preceding sixteen centuries of Christian history – an anachronistic conceptual framework that is ill-suited for the twenty-first century. We find ourselves in "the new post-foreign mission situation," requiring us to reconceive the church and world encounter, not redefine or reform mission. More than ever, mission, its past and future, is in question.

The necessity of transcending the rhetoric of the modern mission movement is critical, given its past associations and its present implications. The historical legacy and modernization of mission call into question the future of the whole enterprise. To return to more biblical language will be an unnerving venture for some. However, through such a risk we acknowledge and embrace the enduring work of God in the past and point toward God's future. Through its long sojourn from the death and resurrection of Jesus to the present day, the gospel has survived all manner of shifts, movements, and traditions. The original impulse of the gospel endures and awaits new expressions. To transcend mission is to hope in the witness of this original impulse for our day and to believe in its power to liberate the men and women who travel though this life with us.

Epilogue: Toward Pilgrim Witness

Imagine a young mother in Kolkata, India. Having suffered the loss of her husband and ensuing destitution for herself and an infant child, she lives on the streets without shelter and with only scraps of food. Those who should have been there for her are unable to help and some have even turned against her. With each passing day, she and her child fall deeper and deeper into despair. She is lost and without hope. As her situation worsens, she cries aloud to the gods for rescue. And yet, rather than getting better, her situation becomes even more grave and hopeless. One night as she sits on the pavement with her listless child in her lap, she looks up to see a man kneeling beside her. Rather than disgust and bother, his eyes are full of compassion and love, and his words are kind and soothing. He says to her, "The Lord, your God, has heard your cries. Your liberation is at hand. The reign of God is in the midst of this city. Find people of peace, and find hope for you and your child."

As day breaks, she sits on the pavement wondering if someone actually spoke to her in the night or if she was dreaming. She hears melodious chants coming from an open door beyond the iron fence on which she is leaning. She gathers her child, rises to her feet, and follows the sounds through the open door. Once inside, she finds a group of white-clad devotees seated in a circle on the floor singing along with tabla drum and cymbals. At one side of the circle of devotees, she sees a figure of an Indian man in a painting. His arms are extended and in his face she recognizes compassion and love. As the singing stops, one of the devotees says, "Come unto me you who are weak and heavy laden, and I will give you rest." She softly mutters, "I need to rest. I want rest." As the chant continues, she weeps.

Conversations with devotees in the group eventually lead to her declaration of Jesus Christ as the true God. From these Christ devotees, she receives food, medicine, and love. She begins meeting with some in their homes and in public spaces. When they gather, they sing songs of devotion, pray to God the Father, Son, and Spirit, and listen to the Holy Scriptures. From the Scriptures, she learns that the one true God as revealed in Jesus Christ desires to establish his reign throughout the earth. She hears that this rule is not far off but near, not just in the future but now, and not dormant but powerful and growing. In the sayings and parables of Jesus, she learns that the rule of God is like a small, obscure seed that is growing in the soil of her city and one day will be as large as a Banyan tree. So, the certainty of God's reign and the expectation of its increase and eventual arrival grow stronger and stronger in her. She talks with devotees about how the reign of God will look when it arrives and prays for its increase in her life, as well as her relatives and friends.

What the young mother comes to realize is that the kingdom of God is unlike any political, military, or governmental rule she has ever known. Rather, the reign of God begins in the mind and heart, works its way into speech and actions, and eventually changes everything about life. As God's reign becomes more prominent, peace, joy, goodness, and patience will characterize her interactions with other devotees as well as friends and neighbors she encounters in the course of her day. Her growing anticipation is that the reign of God will change her neighborhood and city, as it becomes a transforming force in her own life. More and more she realizes that hope does not rest in her position in society, the power of the group of devotees, or even their collective moral force. She remembers how destitute she was before Jesus encountered her, and now she longs for the coming reign of God to transform her life and the life of her daughter. For this young mother, the reign of God is *the* reality for which she lives, *the* source of her hope, and *the* cause to which she gives herself. As a devotee of Jesus, she lives by the words that came to her at the point of deepest need – "The Lord, your God, has heard your cries. Your liberation is at hand."

Whether one is a young mother in Kolkata, a businessman in Hong Kong, a student in the Gambia, a waitress in London, or an engineer in Houston, the story is the same. The reign of God brings transformation and offers hope. Education, privilege, and religion make their promises of hope and liberation, but these do not have the power to transform life and instill hope. True liberation does not come by way of human ingenuity or power, much less a religious tradition. Instead, God declares his power to liberate and transform creation i*n his words* and demonstrates this power *through his deeds.* As mothers, students, and engineers encounter the words and deeds of Jesus, they come to believe the speech and actions of God are more powerful than any other speech and action. His promise is that the kingdoms of this world will give way "to the kingdom of our Lord, and of His Christ; and He will reign forever and ever."

The reign of God is the central narrative, the message of Jesus, and hope for humanity. The coming reign of God is what the Bible is all about, the heart and core of God's plan, and the reason we exist. Mission is not the answer to the problems of young mothers, businessmen, students, and engineers, for those living in India, Africa, or America. At best, mission represents a tradition that grew up around the proclamation of God as Creator and Lord – a means to its end. When mission ascends to status of sacred language, it eclipses the kingdom and thus limits our view of God's reign and muddles our ability to participate in his kingdom. The language of the reign of God, on the other hand, expresses an abiding theme in the Bible that culminates in the message of Jesus. In the reign of God, we discover God and his power, are formed into witnesses and pilgrims, and are liberated and enabled to love those we encounter.

The Kingdom of God

From beginning to end, Scripture narrates the Day of the Lord, the kingdom of God, or the reign of God. The overarching theme from Genesis to the Psalms and in the Prophets is the coming reign of God. At the heart of Jesus' teaching and central to his identity and ministry is the kingdom of God. The apostle Paul proclaims the coming kingdom of God, and John writes of the victory of God's reign. The kingdom of God is vibrant biblical language, and chief among the themes of Scripture.

As Jesus proclaims the kingdom, he confronts evil in all its forms, initiates a way of believing and acting, and eventually gives his life for all humanity. The power of the kingdom of God is a child who becomes the sacrificial Lamb and thereby liberates the world from sin and death. The kingdom is both present and future: it has both arrived and is still to come. The ultimate end is not the sending of messengers but the message of the kingdom of God.

Paul writes of the kingdom of God as the aim of life. Christ's victory over death and resurrection are but "the first fruits," or signs of the liberation to come (1 Cor 15:24). Luke concludes Acts with Paul in Rome under house arrest but still able to testify and preach to all who come to him concerning the kingdom of God (Acts 28:23, 30-31).

The language of Scripture refers to the already-and-coming kingdom of God rather than the mission of God. Rather than preaching mission, advocating for mission, mobilizing for mission, or revising mission, the biblical injunction is to proclaim, promote, and live the kingdom of God. Jesus shows the disciples his pierced hands and feet and then says to them: "Peace be with you; as the Father has sent Me, so I also send you." Jesus' meaning is clear – in the same manner and for the same purpose I was sent, I am sending you. To elevate mission language to the status of sacred language places extra-biblical assumptions and beliefs and a foreign narrative onto Scripture that competes with the kingdom of God. The result is that mission, a modern means, obscures the kingdom of God, the essential reality.

The young mother in Kolkata knows the Creator because of the revealed speech and action of God and the witness to these in Scripture. In these words and deeds, she recognizes the one true God as different from Ganesh, Shiva, and Kali. For an engineer in Houston, God, as revealed through the Bible, is unlike the gods of consumption, hedonism, and nation. For the young mother and the engineer, the language of Scripture contradicts the speech of the modern world. Kingdom language precedes talk about temporal causes, national aspirations, and religious ways, and thus it is distinguishable from all other speech.

Jesus' discourses are full of apocalyptic references. The term "apocalyptic" comes from *apokalypto* or *apokalypsis*, meaning "to uncover" or "to unveil." This vision of God's victory represents the future but also has present effects. As well as being a book of "apocalyptic prophecy," the Book of Revelation is a letter written to encourage specific churches in their day and for their context. Those who received John's Revelation are able to see beyond the power of Rome and view "the world from the heavenly perspective." The disclosure of God's triumph changes the view of present circumstances for the reign of God is the *current* and the *coming* reality that offers *present* and *future* hope.

As a language of hope, the kingdom of God reveals the power of God to intervene in history to make himself present and known as the one who heals, liberates, and transforms. It is the biblical witness through which a young mother discovers God's activity in the world and discerns how she is to participate in the Spirit's work. This discovery and discernment lead to a life of devotion to Christ and gives witness to what she has seen and heard.

The transformative power of the kingdom can be seen in its effect on the apostles and the early church, and their unrelenting proclamation of the reign of God as an alternative view of reality. Embracing the kingdom of God readies us for engagement with the world by transforming us into *witnesses to* the kingdom and *pilgrims of* the kingdom, participating in the coming reign of God.

Witness is both beholding and telling. To *behold* is to witness something that changes one's existence. *Beholding* is to be captured by a vision of that which hopeful and transformative. *Telling* is to convey with one's words and life what has been seen and experienced. Rather than doing or performing witness, we *are* witnesses of what we have beheld of the reign of God. One may speak words of apologetics, doctrine, and mission, but these are not necessarily words of witness. As the young mother from the streets of Kolkata speaks of what she has seen of the power of God and the miracle of transformation in her life, she is a witness.

A vision of the kingdom of God dislocates men and women from temporal hopes and transforms them into people who journey toward a greater vision. Pilgrimage means we join those who live with displacement, expulsion, and separation. The language of pilgrim offers an image of a homeless wanderer exposed to the elements who must rely upon others for basic needs, such as a beggar on the streets of Kolkata, exposed to rain, heat, and mosquitoes, in borrowed spaces and at risk of abuse. A beggar has little-to-no assurance of medical care, food, or security. Asleep at the curb and in alleyways, she may be mistaken for a heap of trash rather than a human being. She is without home, begging for her existence, and outside the structures of power and privilege. Those with power, privilege, money, and means may think that God has preferenced them over those sleeping on the street, when the opposite is the case, but whether in a home or on the street, with ample food or in great hunger, mother or engineer, the ultimate aim of the pilgrim is to be defined by Christ's reign and his way.

Modern-day pilgrims, sojourners, aliens, and strangers are not alone, for these same words describe the people of God in the Old and New Testaments. Followers of Christ are meant to wander as his people have done from the beginning.

Even if displacement is not an actual, physical state, a pilgrim existence is possible. Augustine observes that pilgrimage is the recognition that one is "by grace a pilgrim below, and by grace a citizen above" (15.1). Pilgrimage is the admission that the present is transitory and unstable, and that hope must be for another place of home. Thus, Christendom is not home, and occupation is not the aim. Mission becomes a perversion of pilgrimage when missionaries are viewed as the only true pilgrims while everyone else observes their journey and vicariously participates.

Better Language

Kingdom language prompts those who follow Christ to live as pilgrims who give witness to the coming reign of God. They are not called "missionaries," and their life purpose is not named as "mission." Kingdom language is the better choice of language, because it is rooted in revelation, includes all types of believers, prioritizes formation of life, expands possibilities, underscores the place of the church, liberates from Christendom assumptions, and points to the Spirit's work.

The qualification to be a witness and pilgrim is submission to the reign of God. Witness and pilgrim are not exclusive or narrow occupations that require a special calling or commission. The reign of God, rather than location (mission field) and title (missionary), determine whether one is a witness and pilgrim.

Kingdom language places the end results with what God does, by the means he chooses, and according to his timetable. Mission language, on the other hand, communicates that particular tasks are to be achieved in certain way and measured by a specific matrix. The language of kingdom moves beyond the prescriptions of what *should* happen and opens the possibilities of what *could* happen.

Kingdom language recognizes the place of the community of faith in the activity of God. In the early church, communities of faith emerged in cities and regions and became centers of witness of Christ to those living around them. As Lesslie Newbigin notes, Paul does not establish "in Philippi or in Derbe or in Lystra two organizations, one called the church and the other called the Antioch mission, Lystra branch" (1994:25-26). Rather, ancient churches formed by an encounter with God exist in particular locales as expressions of the Spirit's witness in their corner of the world. As the Spirit speaks to the church (Acts 13:1), the witness of the Spirit is extended into adjoining, as well as far-away regions. The example from Scripture is that witness spreads from local communities of faith, as believers move through their neighborhoods, across the city, and into the world.

Mission, on the other hand, extracts individuals from churches and diverts them into mission organizations to give witness as missionaries. Through the transfer of its witness, the place and purpose of these churches are subverted. The obvious conclusion is that mission organizations must exist, because the church is inadequate. While the church is far from perfect and often too modern, its calling is to be a witnessing, pilgriming community, as it continually reorients its life toward the reign of God. If the church is inadequate, the antidote is surrender to and formation in the reign of God, not mission.

The answer for some is to combine church and mission. If the church is inadequate, it is because it lacks mission in its essence or substance. The corrective is to define the church *as* mission. Emil Brunner is often quoted in this regard: "The Church exists by mission, just as a fire exists by burning. Where there is no mission, there is no Church; and where there is neither Church nor mission, there is no faith" (108). Yet those who quote Brunner's words do not acknowledge his nuanced use of mission and that his ultimate emphasis is on the proclamation of the gospel. Rather than mission, it seems more appropriate to say the church exists by the power of the Spirit for its witness to the coming reign of God.

The kingdom of God serves as a constant reminder that the church is not a privileged society or club, but a sojourning people who give witness to God who controls and sustains all things. The empowerment of the Spirit initiates the expansion of the church from Jerusalem to the corners of the world. This promised power of the Spirit becomes witness as the reign of God arrives in the lives of ordinary people.

Post-Mission Encounters

Imagine a man named Jack, in his early 40s, who works for an engineering firm in Houston. Jack and his wife, Sarah, have two children and live in a middle-class, suburban neighborhood. Their lives are busy with work, weekend activities, and civic responsibilities. Although Jack's life is full of activity, he is numbed by it all. He feels that life is going nowhere and that there must surely be something more to life. He gets up, goes to work, comes home, mows the yard, goes to soccer practice with the kids, and takes his annual vacation. The routine and grind seem to be pointless. It is not that life is hard or that they are destitute, but it is empty. His numbness grows into anxiety and personal crisis. The internal struggle reaches such a point that one afternoon he blurts out to his wife that he is quitting his job and changing his life. Both are standing in the kitchen, she at the sink and he at the table. She immediately turns off the tap and looks at him in disbelief. "I want more out of life, too," she says, "but throwing away all that we have worked for and putting our family and home at risk is not the answer." Their exchange becomes heated and accusations are made in both directions. Finally, Jack storms out of the house, gets in his car, and drives out of the city. After an hour of aimless driving, he stops at a small, roadside diner. As he sits at the counter with a cup of coffee, he says to himself, "I am trapped in this job – in this life. I need to know that life is about more than money, a mortgage, and work. I need some hope that there is something more."

An older, greying man behind the counter can't help but hear Jack, and asks, "What's up?" Jack does not hesitate but tells him everything – his feelings of being trapped, the emptiness of the routine, the encounter with Sarah, and his desperation to know his life is more than the endless, numbing routine of work. He cannot stop talking as he unloads all of this on a complete stranger. Once Jack has said everything he can, he looks at the waiter confused and embarrassed.

The man behind the counter gives Jack a slight smile and says, "I was right where you are four years ago – trying to make sense of everything. I gave up a good job at an investment firm, moved to a smaller house, and in the process nearly ruined my marriage. For me, it was about destitute people on the streets of Houston and the feeling that I had to do something about it. I tried to solve the injustice and inequality, but in no time at all, I found myself spent and wondering if I was making any difference. After working for a nonprofit for a year, I left disillusioned because of a conflict with a fellow worker and confused by the politics of it all." He paused for a moment and then continued. "I thought maybe religion might be the answer. I had grown up in the church and knew the lingo but was not sure what all of it meant. I had heard people talk about being a missionary as the ultimate form of sacrifice and doing mission work as the ultimate way of service. So, I talked my wife into going down that road. We considered becoming missionaries and moving to Brazil, but once I started making enquiries and even began the application process with a mission agency, I knew being a missionary was not who we are and mission was not the answer for us."

He stopped, looked toward the street for moment, and then at Jack. "I became so desperate to know why I existed and what I was to do that I began to question if there was any meaning to life and if I should go on living. I came to the end of myself and my way of putting it all together. I had never really read the Bible. Oh, I heard it read in church and heard plenty of sermons from the Bible, but I had not read it for myself. So, I decided I would give it a try. I began reading from the beginning of the New Testament searching for an answer – some kind of answer. I noticed immediately Jesus talking a lot about the kingdom of God. It jumped off the page and grabbed me. I had read of the kingdom of God before but had not really *seen* it. The kingdom of God and kingdom of heaven were everywhere, and I began to connect with kingdom words. Over a period of time and after loads of discussion with friends, I began to understand that the kingdom was Jesus' thing. I discovered that the point of Christianity is not church attendance, or me being a moral person, or about me getting something from God or doing for God. It is about God's reign coming to my life and spreading throughout my family, my city, and the world. Once I understood this, I started on a journey that has taken me in a direction I could have never imagined. The details of my life are still not settled; in fact, they may be a bit more messy, but I am sure of the direction."

The waiter paused again for a long time, looked down at his hands on the counter, and then back up at Jack. "I believe that God is up to something in and around me, in this town – in the world. My life is meant to coincide with what he is doing to establish his reign in the systems, situations, and lives around me. I don't have to make sense of how this will happen. In fact, I can't make sense of it. What I must do is believe that he is at work and yield myself to him. Life now is like a trip into the new world of God and his activities. I exist for the ride and to tell those I meet along the way what I am seeing and experiencing. It is like this: God wants to bring sense to this crazy, dysfunctional world, and he wants to do it as he makes sense of my crazy, dysfunctional life." Jack had heard everything the man behind the counter had said. But more than hearing, he could see that the man had found an answer – a life altering answer.

Jack's story of anxiety and emptiness is more than an imagined narrative. Many caught in the shift of the landscape of modern life know a similar loss of meaning and are looking for hope. Their questions demand more than a pat answer or a static, one-dimensional response. They need to take a journey – a pilgrimage – that is dynamic and expansive. The reign of God offers men and women meaning and hope and beckons them to travel new pathways in the changing landscape.

Kingdom language allows a waiter to speak to an engineer of more than church-talk but also matters that encompass the whole of creation – the social, economic, ecological, and political dimensions of life. By its nature, the kingdom of God encompasses the whole of creation and thus provides the intersection that touches every corner of life, redeeming the crises that exist within modern men and women by pointing them to the transformative power of the Spirit. Mission language can try to do this but fails because it does not have the capacity or the force to respond to the current social and spiritual landscape.

The reign of God has a history of creating wild and varied possibilities. The story of the Christian movement is that God continually moves his pilgrim people in new ways to bear witness to his reign through a variety of means. The role of the pilgrim witness is to watch what God does in and around him or her and to continually ask: What could God do in my life, through my presence in this place? This kind of expectation is more probable when the language of the kingdom is front and center. With such language, men and women are primed to move at the Spirit's prompting, though with possibly fewer people and far less fanfare. Pilgrimage offers the possibility of participation with the Spirit in witness to the world.

The transformation of a young mother and an engineer begins with an encounter but continues throughout their lives. The process of transformation for both does not center in a religion that conquers, ideas that originate in the West, or through civilizational uplift. Rather their encounter with the kingdom of God as revealed in Jesus Christ transforms who they are and how they will act throughout the course of their lives. The reign of God means they live as pilgrims in the way of the kingdom, and they give witness to family and friends of the kingdom's power to confront and transform. The reign of God will manifest itself in their conversations and choices. As pilgrims, they give witness as they go. However, their going may or may not be of their choice but as migrants, or because of employment, displacement, political partition, or ethnic cleansing. Historically these have caused pilgrims to move from place to place. Opportunities in work may open the option of going to a new city or a different country. The need for work may mandate a move to a new place. Or, a community of faith in Kolkata or Houston may hear the Spirit say, "Send a young mother in your midst to the other side of the city," or, "Support an engineer who is being transferred by his company to Afghanistan." The crux of the matter lies not in the sending or the going but in the reign of God that converts men and women into pilgrim witnesses. The testimony of Scripture and the story of the church are of the kingdom of God that has come and keeps coming as people are transformed by people who are continually being transformed by the power of God's reign.

Selected Works

Adomanán. 1995. *Life of St Columba*. Translated by Richard Sharpe. Middlesex, England: Penguin Books.

Atwood, Craig D. 2004. *Community of the Cross: Moravian Piety in Colonial Bethlehem*. University Park, PA: The Pennsylvania State University Press.

Augustine. 1984. *Concerning the City of God Against the Pagans*. Translated by Henry Bettenson. London: Penguin Books.

Bangert, William V. 1986. *A History of the Society of Jesus*. St. Louis, MO: Institute of Jesuit Sources.

Banks, Louis Albert. 1889. "Carey's Missionary World and Ours." *Zion's Herald* (1868-1910).

Barr, James. 1961. *The Semantics of Biblical Languages*. Oxford: Oxford University Press.

Barram, Michael. 2007. "The Bible, Mission, and Social Location: Toward a Missional Hermeneutic." *Interpretation* 61, no. 1:42-58.

Barnett, Paul. 2008. *Paul: Missionary of Jesus*. After Jesus, Vol. 2. Grand Rapids, MI: William B. Eerdmans.

Bartlett, Robert. 1993. *The Making of Europe: Conquest, Colonization and Cultural Change, 950-1350*. Princeton, NJ: Princeton University Press.

Bede, The Venerable. 1969. *Ecclesiastical History of the English People*. Oxford Medieval Texts. Oxford: Clarendon Press.

Bediako, Kwame. 2004. *Jesus and the Gospel in Africa: History and Experience*. Maryknoll, NY: Orbis Books.

Bellarmine, Roberto Francesco Romolo. 2015. *De Notis Ecclesia/On the Marks of the Church*. Translated by Ryan Grant. United States: Mediatrix Press.

Bosch, David. 2011. *Transforming Mission: Paradigm Shifts in Theology of Mission*. Maryknoll, NY: Orbis Books.

Brown, Peter Robert Lamont. 1996. *The Rise of Western Christendom: Triumph and Diversity*, AD 200-1000. Cambridge, MA: Blackwell.

Bruce, F. F. 1958. *The Spreading Flame: The Rise and Progress of Christianity from Its First Beginnings to the Conversion of the English*. Grand Rapids, MI: William B. Eerdmans.

Brunner, Emil. 1931. *The Word and the World*. London: SCM Press.

Carver, William. 1909. *Missions in the Plan of the Ages: Bible Studies in Missions*. New York: Fleming H. Revell.

Cerfaux, Lucien. 1960. *Apostle and Apostolate According to the Gospel of St. Matthew*. Translated by Donald D. Duggan. New York: Desclee Company.

Cipolla, Carlo M. 1970. *European Culture and Overseas Expansion*. Middlesex, England: Penguin Books.

Clossey, Luke. 2008. *Salvation and Globalization in the Early Jesuit Missions*. New York: Cambridge University Press.

Dalmases, Cándido de. 1985. *Ignatius of Loyola, Founder of the Jesuits: His Life and Works*. Translated by Jerome Aixalá. St. Louis, MO: The Institute of Jesuit Sources.

DuBose, Francis M. 1983. *God Who Sends: A Fresh Quest for Biblical Mission*. Nashville, TN: Broadman Press.

Dykes, J. Oswald. 1890. "The Modern Missionary Movement." *Baptist Missionary Magazine* (1873-1909).

Eddy, Sherwood. 1945. *Pathfinders of the World Missionary Crusade*. New York: Abingdon-Cokesbury Press.

Escobar, Samuel. 2000. "Evangelical Missiology: Peering Into the Future at the Turn of the Century." In *Global Missiology for the 21st Century: The Iguassu Dialogue*, edited by William D. Taylor, pp. 101-22. Grand Rapids, MI: Baker Academic.

Finnegan, Charles V. 1994. "Franciscans and the 'New Evangelization.'" *Spirit and Life: A Journal of Contemporary Franciscanism* 6:1-6.

Foster, John. 1939. *The Church of the T'ang Dynasty*. London: Society for Promoting Christian Knowledge.

Fulcher of Chartres. 1971. "Deeds of the Franks on Their Pilgrimage to Jerusalem." In *The First Crusade: The Chronicle of Fulcher of Chartres and Other Source Materials*, edited by Edward Peters, pp. 24-90. Philadelphia, PA: University of Pennsylvania Press.

Glover, Robert H. 1946. *The Bible Basis of Missions*. Chicago, IL: Moody Press.

Gregory. 2004. *The Letters of Gregory the Great*. Translated by John R. C. Martyn. 3 volumes. Mediaeval Sources in Translation 40. Toronto: Pontifical Institute of Mediaeval Studies.

Guibert, Joseph de. 1964. *The Jesuits: Their Spiritual Doctrine and Practice: A Historical Study*. Translated by William J. Young. Chicago, IL: Institute of Jesuit Sources.

Harnack, Adolf. 1962. *The Mission and Expansion of Christianity in the First Three Centuries*. New York: Harper.

Hastings, Adrian. 1999. "150-500." In *A World History of Christianity*, edited by Adrian Hastings, pp. 25-65. Grand Rapids, MI: William B. Eerdmans.

Huhtinen, Pekka, and Gregory Lockwood. 2001. "Luther and World Missions: A Review." *Concordia Theological Quarterly* 65, no. 1:15-29.

Humphreys, David. 1969. *An Historical Account of the Incorporated Society for the Propagation of the Gospel in Foreign Parts*. New York: Arno Press.

Ignatius Loyola. 1970. *The Constitutions of the Society of Jesus*. Translated by George E Ganss. St. Louis, MO: Institute of Jesuit Sources.

_______. 1992. *The Autobiography of St. Ignatius Loyola*. Translated by Joseph F. O'Callaghan. New York: Fordham University Press.

Irvin, Dale T. 1998. *Christian Histories, Christian Traditioning: Rendering Accounts*. Maryknoll, NY: Orbis Books.

Jenkins, Philip. 2008. *The Lost History of Christianity: The Thousand-Year Golden Age of the Church in the Middle East, Africa, and Asia-and How It Died*. New York: HarperOne.

Kaiser, Walter. 2000. *Mission in the Old Testament: Israel as a Light to the Nations*. Grand Rapids, MI: Baker Books.

Kollman, Paul. 2011. "At the Origins of Mission and Missiology: A Study in the Dynamics of Religious Language." *Journal of the American Academy of Religion* 79, no. 2:425-58.

Latourette, Kenneth Scott. 1936. *Missions Tomorrow*. New York: Harper & Brothers.

______. 1970. *A History of the Expansion of Christianity*. 7 volumes. Grand Rapids, MI: Zondervan Publishing House.

Laymen's Foreign Missions Inquiry. 1933. New York: Harper & Brothers.

Love, Julian Price. 1941. *The Missionary Message of the Bible*. New York: Macmillan.

Luther, Martin. 1970. *Luther's Work*, Volume 39: *Church and Ministry I*. Edited by Eric W. Gritsch. Philadelphia, PA: Fortress Press.

Macquarrie, John. 1963. *Twentieth-Century Religious Thought*. New York: Harper & Row.

Márkus, Gilbert. 1999. "Iona: Monks, Pastors and Missionaries." In *Spes Scotorum, Hope of the Scots: Saint Columba, Iona and Scotland*, edited by Dauvit Broun and Thomas Owen Clancy, pp. 115-38. Edinburgh: T. & T. Clark.

McBeth, Leon. 1987. *The Baptist Heritage*. Nashville, TN: Broadman Press.

McKeon, Richard. 1987. *Rhetoric: Essays in Invention and Discovery*. Woodbridge, CT: Ox Bow Press.

Muirchú. 2005. "The Vita Patricii by Muirchú." In *Discovering Saint Patrick*, translated by Thomas O'Loughlin, pp. 192-229. London: Darton, Longman & Todd.

Neill, Stephen C. 1959. *Creative Tension*. London: Edinburgh House Press.

______. 1984. *A History of Christianity in India: The Beginning to AD 1707*. Cambridge: Cambridge University Press.

______. 1986. *A History of Christian Missions*. 2nd Edition. London: Penguin Books.

Newbigin, Lesslie. 1958. *One Body, One Gospel, One World: The Christian Mission Today*. London: Wm. Carling & Co.

______. 1977. "The Future of Missions and Missionaries." *Review & Expositor* 74, no. 2, 209-18.

______. 1994. *A Word in Season: Perspectives on Christian World Missions*. Grand Rapids, MI: William B. Eerdmans.

O'Malley, John W. 1994. "Mission and the Early Jesuits." *Ignatian Spirituality and Mission: The Way Supplement* 79:3-10.

Payne, Ernest A. 1942. *The Church Awakes: The Story of the Modern Missionary Movement*. London: The Carey Press.

Pratt, Zane G., M. David Sills, and Jeff K. Walters. 2014. *Introduction to Global Missions*. Nashville, TN: B&H Publishing Group.

Re-Thinking Missions: *A Laymen's Inquiry After One Hundred Years*. 1932. New York: Harper & Brothers.

Riley-Smith, Jonathan. 1980. "Crusading as an Act of Love." *History* 65 (1980):177-92.

______. 1987. *The Crusades: A Short History*. New Haven, CT: Yale University Press.

Rowley, H. H. 1945. *The Missionary Message of the Old Testament*. London: Carey Press.

Stott, John R. W. 1975. *Christian Mission in the Modern World*. Downers Grove, IL: InterVarsity Press.

Thompson, James. 1903. *The Decline of the Missi Dominici in Frankish Gaul*. Chicago, IL: The University of Chicago Press.

Townsend, John T. 1986. "Missionary Journeys in Acts and European Missionary Societies." *Anglican Theological Review* 68, no. 2:99-104.

Tyerman, Christopher. 2004. *Fighting for Christendom: Holy War and the Crusades*. Oxford: Oxford University Press.

Walls, Andrew F. 1991. "Structural Problems in Mission Studies." *International Bulletin of Missionary Research* 15, no. 4:146-55.

______. 2001. "The Eighteenth-Century Protestant Missionary Awakening in Its European Context." In *Christian Missions and the Enlightenment*, edited by Brian Stanley, pp. 22-44. Studies in the History of Christian Missions. Grand Rapids, MI: William B. Eerdmans.

______. 2002. "Eusebius Tries Again: The Task of Reconceiving and Re-Visioning the Study of Christian History." In *Enlarging the Story: Perspectives on Writing World Christian History*, edited by Wilbert R. Shenk, pp. 1-21. Maryknoll, NY: Orbis Books.

Warneck, Gustav. 1901. *Outline of a History of Protestant Missions from the Reformation to the Present Time*. New York: Fleming H. Revell.

Webb, Diana. 2002. *Medieval European Pilgrimage, c.700-c.1500*. European Culture and Society. New York: Palgrave.

Welz, Justinian von. 1969. *Justinian Welz: Essays by an Early Prophet of Missions*. Edited by James A. Scherer. Christian World Mission Books. Grand Rapids, MI: William B. Eerdmans.

Williams, Joel F. 2012. "The Missionary Message of the New Testament." In *Discovering the Mission of God: Best Missional Practices of the 21st Century*, edited by Mike Barnett and Robin Martin, pp. 49-67. Downers Grove, IL: InterVarsity Press.

Wood, Ian. 2001. *The Missionary Life: Saints and the Evangelisation of Europe, 400-1050*. Harlow, England: Longman.

World Missionary Conference, 1910: The History and Records of the Conference Together with Addresses Delivered at the Evening Meetings. 9 volumes. Edinburgh: Oliphant, Anderson, & Ferrier.

Wright, Christopher J. H. 2006. *The Mission of God: Unlocking the Bible's Grand Narrative*. Downers Grove, IL: IVP Academic.

Zinzendorf, Nicolaus Ludwig. 1963. *Hauptschriften*, edited by Erich Beyreuther and Gerhard Meyer, Volume 3. Hildesheim, Germany: Georg Olms Verlagsbuchhandlung.